TELLING TALES OUT OF SCHOOL

by Christine Clack Lusk

Myrtle —
May you
enjoy and smile!
Love you,
Chris Lusk

TELLING TALES OUT OF SCHOOL

by Christine Clack Lusk

Memories from my 30 years of teaching

...with comments about

WHAT WAS RIGHT WITH OUR SCHOOLS
in the '50s, '60s and '70s

ISBN: 1-58721-194-7

1st Books rev. 6/19/00

ABOUT THE BOOK

It covers the years of the '50's 60's and '70's, with comments about, "What Was Right With Our Schools". With so much press and talk about the deterioration of our schools, this book points out vividly what the author feels used to be right (not perfect) but certainly right about our schools.

She states that it is true-life stories and personal reminiscences of years gone by. It is in no way a complete autobiography, just her memories, impressions and perceptions of these phases in her teaching career. Being a child of the Great Depression, it shows how an insignificant farm girl became a teacher. It includes her thoughts on teaching which she learned by trial and error. Included are humorous incidents of many students, confessions and other interesting information. Also included are numerous "bloopers" made by the teacher. This included the year that integration came to the south.

It has been critiqued by a staff member of LSU in Baton Rouge, Louisiana. He states he can detect historical and educational value (especially for high school teachers and students) as well as humor. Of course, most of her former students will enjoy it as it includes tales about many of them.

TABLE OF CONTENTS

Memories from my
30 years of teaching

by Christine Clack Lusk

...with comments about

WHAT WAS RIGHT WITH OUR SCHOOLS
in the '50s, '60s and '70s

*With so much press and talk about the
deterioration of our schools, this book will point
out vividly what I feel used to be right (not
perfect), but certainly right about our schools.*

Dedications:

-to my parents, Mr. and Mrs. Thomas I. Clack, who
sacrificed to see that I received my college degree

-to my husband Bo and sons Daryl and Larry, whose love
and cooperation made it possible for me to have two careers

-and lastly, to all my former students, each of whom have
left *footprints on my heart*

Special thanks:

-to Toni Newton, a former student, for arranging my notes
and putting them into book format for me

-to Robin Fontenot, another former student, for helping to
input the text into the computer

-to Joyce and Jason Walker, my sister and nephew, who
helped me with the "King's English" and dotted my i's and
crossed my t's

Pictures from the Past...

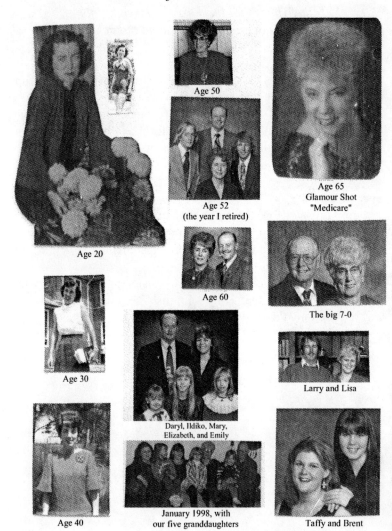

Age 20

Age 50

Age 52
(the year I retired)

Age 65
Glamour Shot
"Medicare"

Age 30

Age 60

The big 7-0

Larry and Lisa

Daryl, Ildiko, Mary,
Elizabeth, and Emily

Age 40

January 1998, with
our five granddaughters

Taffy and Brent

INTRODUCTION

It has been said that to teach is to touch a child's heart forever--but I say that to teach is to have your own heart touched!

"To every thing there is a season, and a time to every purpose under the heaven." (Ecclesiastes 3:1) Through the seasons of my life, I have had many treasured memories and enjoyed many things. My, how sweet to hold my own babies and what an awesome gift were our five granddaughters, who quickly became the "apples of my eye." They have added a whole new dimension to my life! Bo always wished for grandsons--but became absolute putty in a little girl's hands.

I believe every event in one's life is a thread weaving a pattern that unfolds by design. This thought brings to mind the plight of the bumble bee: "According to recognized aeronautical tests, the bumble bee cannot fly because of the shape and weight of his body in relation to his total wing area. The bumble bee doesn't know this--so he goes ahead and flies anyway!"

If the bumble bee can accomplish such a remarkable feat--maybe, just maybe, I can write this book!

Yes, I have reached the big "7-0" and Bo and I recently celebrated our 45th anniversary. I've also bleached my hair *au naturel*. I simply got tired of the weekly rinse and the occasional "blue tint." Neither of my sons really liked it and Bo's comment was, "Well, I can't lose you in the crowd!" I haven't decided if that was a compliment or not! My teenage granddaughter, who can be brutally frank, says that she likes it and I've also received many compliments from others.

With age, I have acquired a new appreciation for the autumn years of one's life. I have found that life is a climb uphill--the farther up, the broader the horizon and the more wonderful the view of life. Years of autumn can be worn with a dignity that reveals richness and beauty far exceeding the passing flowers of spring. Actually, I plan to never get old--just older. Think about it!

This brings to mind a beautiful poem given to me by Mrs.

Gladys Holmes my friend who has taught many of you. She said it was one of her favorites and it certainly has become a favorite of mine.

LET ME GROW LOVELY
By Karle Wilson Baker

Let me grow lovely growing old--
So many fine things do:
Laces and ivory and gold,
And silks need not be new;
And there is healing in old trees,
Old streets a glamour hold;
Why may not I, as well as these,
Grow lovely, growing old?

I still live in the sleepy little village of Epps, Louisiana, where Bogzack meanders lazily on the western side. We still have only one traffic light, but we recently got a new first-class post office. We also have a Community Center and Town Hall Complex which has facilities for small gatherings. We recently lost our branch bank, but another bank is now building a facility. In recent years, we have also become the gateway to Poverty Point State Commemorative Area, a major archaeological find dating from before the time of Moses. Recently the date has been determined to be between 1800-1850 B.C.

Epps and Pioneer schools are consolidated at Epps, grades 9-12. School life has changed in so many ways that I have no regrets for taking an early retirement. I retired in 1979 with 30 years of teaching experience. My son Larry graduated the same year. I overheard him say, "It only took me 18 years to graduate, but it took my Mom 30. Now does that tell you anything?" Bro. Pat Lofton, my pastor, said, "Chris enjoyed teaching, but retired as she had enjoyed all she could stand!"

I have found that retirement is that time of life when you are too busy to do any of the things you planned to do when you thought you would have the time. I feel sure I would have missed school--I did love teaching--but my first granddaughter arrived in September of 1980, so I never actually regretted retiring. If I ever felt guilty about not cooking for my family, I made up for it during the first few years of retirement. Actually, I have always felt *recycled*, not retired.

After I retired, the job offers came! But I had not relaxed enough at the time they came. Actually, I needed to recharge my batteries as I was beginning to hear the roar of the typewriters. Upon retirement, the job offers included: secretary-treasurer of the West Carroll Parish Police Jury, business education teacher at Sam Crow Academy in Oak Grove, work in the tax assessor's office, and also work in a lawyer's office in Oak Grove. I was also offered a job through the Vocational School at Lake Providence to begin in August in Epps. A job was offered to me by the boat plant in Delhi; I was recommended by a friend. Lloyd Neal wanted me to help keep books for his farm, and Don Raley, a former student of mine, offered me the most enticing job of all: he wanted me to become his bookkeeper and to just name my hours and days to work. All of the above job offers were certainly flattering (I did not apply for any of them); they just happened too soon after retirement.

Before I begin to reminisce, I'd like to quote Proverbs 25:11: "A word fitly spoken is like apples of gold in pictures of silver." To me, encouragement was better than too much criticism and I diligently tried to put this wise proverb to good use. Through my years of teaching, I tried to use this verse to inspire me to always encourage those I taught. I learned not to crush a student's spirit when he failed, to never compare him with others who outshone him, to encourage him to do better for himself, and to grant him the greatest of all satisfactions, the pleasure that comes with personal accomplishment.

I learned that you receive more respect when you do not set yourself up as the epitome of perfection. Never be afraid to admit it when you really don't know; too err is human and teachers are human too! I've always loved this saying" "A teacher is one who pretends to have known all his life what he just learned yesterday."

With so many of my planned hobbies on hold (I had planned to do more needlepoint, take art and piano lessons and travel), I want to tell you how this book idea came about. You may also be interested to know that I never planned to teach. Both more or less evolved, really by accident. These were two serendipitous events in more ways than one!

First, let me tell you about becoming a teacher. In reflecting on my past, I recall that as a little girl playing, I always insisted on being the teacher. Just bossy, I guess!

I graduated from Rayville High School in Rayville, Louisiana, at the age of 16 with a grade point average of 3.7, placing second in a class of 73. The scholarship I received allowed me to attend LSU in Baton Rouge, Louisiana. I planned to go into the field of business, majoring in business, or commerce, as it was then called. My plans were to work in the field of business, certainly not to teach.

During World War II, there was a teacher shortage. My former principal, Mr. R.S. Hargis, asked me to fill in temporarily in the business department for him. I certainly could have used the money, so after only three years of college, I taught at RHS, my alma mater, for two years. My first year was the class of 1947. To them, and to the class of 1948, I give much credit for my becoming a teacher. I was young, inexperienced, and had a great deal to learn. I found that I truly enjoyed teenagers and usually related well to them.

In retrospect, I did so many things wrong. For example, the first day of typing class, I had the students sit calmly and quietly and listen to me list all the parts of the typewriter and their uses. That's just one of the examples of the many things I did wrong. I quickly learned the truth of this principle: "Tell me and I forget; show me and I remember; involve me and I understand." I soon learned that they needed hands-on experience. Many of my students will remember that first day when I very quickly taught a few correct reaches, enough to type "This is fun." We actually took one or two speed tests. You may be wondering how this ties in with my becoming a teacher. The students could have given me such a hard time and made my life so miserable that I would have never wanted to enter a classroom again. But, bless them, they made teaching fun for me, and really because of the cooperation of the RHS classes of 1947 and 1948, I decided to become qualified to teach. My hat's off to them, and at several reunions, I've told them so! By the way, during this first year of teaching, I had charge of 180 students: four classes of typing, one of bookkeeping and a last period study hall. That was really an experience I shall never forget!

Now, let me tell you about this book and how it evolved. Douglas Fairchild and Toni Newton, among others, were in attendance at the summer reunion of 1996. Through the years, many class reunions have been held and the students usually invite all of their former teachers. I always have a ball. This one was no exception! Those of you who knew Douglas in school will remember him as the class clown. Well, he has never grown up and probably never will! I see him at church each Sunday and with the blessing of both Bo and his wife, he proceeds to give me a big bear hug. He says that he could not do that in school and is making up for lost time! He then looks at Bo and tells him that hug should last me till next Sunday. See what I mean?

At the '96 reunion, he had each class member and teacher come forward to say a few words. My turn came, and upon returning to my seat, I remembered that I had forgotten something I wanted to say. So I raised my hand, waved to him, and was completely ignored. Finally, I called out to him and he said, as he videotaped the entire program, "I wish that young lady in the back would please sit down and shut up!" He said he had waited 40 years to tell me that! So then the fun began with remember this, remember that! I finally remarked in joking, "You'd better be careful what you say as I'm planning to write a book and I'm going to name names and simply tell all." I also said, "I even have the title for it, *Tales Out of School!*" All of this was a joke on my part, but many started encouraging me to do just that. After the reunion, the incident was completely forgotten by me, but I received a letter from Toni thanking me for the tools I had given her which are the foundation for much of the work she does now. She offered to put my memoirs into book format and suggested that I start putting together a manuscript.

The more I thought about it, the more little memories began

to "pop" into my mind, and I thought it really might be fun. The planned hobbies could remain on hold and I decided that I'd better do this while I still have a little memory left. If I had planned to write a book from the beginning of my teaching career, I would have jotted down a few things and kept all my mementos. I have a few, but through the years many have been lost or misplaced. That is why I ask each of you to please not be offended at what I may or may not remember. I believe each of you will realize the "old girl" is not as young as she used to be.

In fact, Daryl and Larry have noticed that Bo and I have become more thoughtful, more reflective and quieter than we used to be. They say we give them more of an opportunity to talk. The truth is that we're both sitting there going through the alphabet trying to remember names of their friends to inquire about! Sometimes when you hit a letter the name jumps out of your subconscious. My mother never told me it would be like this! Maybe it was because she couldn't remember what it was she was supposed to tell me not to forget. *(Paraphrased from "On Forgetting," author unknown.)*

Fred Allen said, "I always have trouble remembering three things: faces, names, and I can't remember what the third thing is."

I have always loved this saying. "When you do not want to remember some incident, simply say "I distinctly remember that I forgot that!"

And now…

Class,
may I
have
your
attention!

COME JOIN THE JOURNEY
(My 30 Years of Teaching)

REFLECTIONS OF RAYVILLE
(1947-1948)

Rayville High School

RHS Hornets
Colors: Green and Gold

"Reflect upon your present blessings of which every man has plenty; not on your past misfortunes, of which all men have some."
Charles Dickens

PRESTIGIOUS PRINCIPAL
Mr. R.S. Hargis

Mr. R.S. Hargis was a prestigious gentleman if I've ever known one. He was friendly in a reserved kind of way, a man of few words and respected by all. Many simply stood in awe of him. He wore rubber-soled shoes and could be right by your side before you knew it.

He had been my own high school principal and I admired him very much. To work on his faculty as a teacher was quite an experience for me. I actually got to go into his inner office, which students referred to as the "inner sanctum." Only those students who misbehaved were ever "privileged" to enter this door.

He always was helpful to me and gave me the respect due any teacher. For that I will always be grateful.

INTRIGUING INFORMATION AND INCIDENTAL INCIDENTS
(Reminiscing)

In doing a little research, I discovered that I taught 180 students in 1947, more than in any other year of my entire teaching career. In 1948, I taught 126 students, which was also more than I ever had in any later year.

In 1947 and for many years thereafter, a student had to get 40 words a minute on speed tests or receive only half credit for the course. Maybe I shouldn't list those who received only half credit in typing, but I have a reason for doing so. In 1947, students receiving half credit (meaning they did not average 40 words per minute on speed tests) were: David Richardson, Billy Dew, Marie Calloway, Jerry Meeks,* W.C. Stockton, Vida Mae Williamson, James Abrams, Ray Calloway, Ruby Kee, Louise Rainer and Markaye Cooper. *Notice the asterisk by Jerry Meeks' name.*

At a recent reunion of this class, a tall, good-looking guy entered the room. All eyes turned for he had not attended a reunion before. Of course, I went to say hello and to introduce my husband to him. Before Bo and a few others, he told me that he had a confession to make. He had thought I was the cutest thing and wanted to be in my class again, so he deliberately failed his speed test so he could repeat the course. "Yes, of course," I said, never for a minute really believing him. I used my usual comment when given a compliment: "I'm sorry, that's worth an "A" but I don't have my grade book with me." That night when I got home, I retrieved my grade books (I somehow managed to keep all 30 of them) and discovered that Jerry was really telling the truth. He had done just that. Jerry Meeks, I didn't know you cared! Just recently, while attending the 50th reunion of this class of '48, James Abrams confessed to me that he had done the same thing. I checked my grade book and sure enough he too had done just that!

In 1948, to be fair, those students who failed to receive a 40 word per minute average and received half credit were: Donald Faust, Tootsie Myrick, Helen Pettit, Lola Oliver, Dorothy McHand, Paul Hammett, Mary Sue Gryder and Reggie Thomason.

Now to compliment a few! The names listed below made an A for their semester grade. If an asterisk (*) appears after a name, he/she had an A for both semesters. In 1947, in bookkeeping they were: Geraldine Burkett,* Elaine Jones, Lilwin Newsom,* Frank Vineyard,* Betty Phillips,* Ellie Morgan, Yvonne Netherland and Evelyn Trumbo.

In typing, they were: Ray Thompson,* Howard Jordan, Marvin Kemp, Marjorie Prine, Evelyn Trumbo,* Claydeen Clack,* Gerald Ray Donald,* Kathleen Hopkins,* Jackie Fletcher,* Bobbie Grantham, Royce Johnson, Myristine McNease, Jean Bruce, Olive Ann Doughty and Billy Jefferies.

In 1948, students making A's in bookkeeping were James Burkett,* Betty Stoecker, James Abrams, Mildred Hall and Arvie Jackson.

In shorthand, they were: Alma Lester, Ora Bell McHand.

In typing: James Abrams, Earline Brown,* Ned Brunson, Ted Brunson, Loree Dampier,* Sammie Davis,* Anna Mae Nance, Nedra Posey,* Evel Lee Prine, Irvin Earl Sorey, Charles Clark, James Burkett,* Opal Jackson,* Jeanette Jones,* Mary

Kolb, Jerry Meeks, David Richardson, Patsy Scogin,* Roy Statham, W.C. Stockton, Vida Mae Williamson, Wendell Holloway, Pauline Price* and Ray Calloway.

Nancy Hunt has told me on more than one occasion that she simply does not know what she would have done if she had not learned typing skills from me. She married young and had small children to support. During the war, she was able to get a job typing. She says she will always be grateful for the skills she learned in my class.

I believe Ruby Kee started her career in banking right out of high school. I recently learned that Patsy Scogin became a business education major and teacher and has recently retired. She was one of my better students!

Betty Graham, a student, became my substitute teacher the year I had the mumps at age 21. I received many notes from my students hoping that I was having a "swell" time. I wish I had kept some of them. I had measles and missed my own high school graduation. I honestly think my mother grabbed me and ran when she heard of a childhood disease.

W.B. "Dub" Summer took typing from me in 1948. He eventually married a girl from Epps where I later taught: Betty Lou Nelson, called "Pete" (My Adorable Imp). As my retirement drew near, I planned to spend time outdoors on my patio where a very crooked light pole was in plain view. I knew he had "pull" with Louisiana Power and Light Company where he worked--so I called him and sure enough I now have a very straight pole in my backyard. It was installed on a day when I was not at home, and a man said to my mother-in-law who lived next door, "I wonder if that lady knows what this is costing LP&L." To Dub I will always be grateful. I'm not a perfectionist, but that crooked pole bothered me as do uneven pictures, blinds, etc.

Remember what I previously said about our principal wearing rubber-soled shoes? One day he appeared in my room with one of my students and asked me if I would give the student permission to return to my study hall. The tall boy (I can't remember who) started back to his seat, no doubt thinking that he had gotten off rather easy. But Mr. Hargis, in his own manner of discipline, said, "No, I mean return to your seat the same way you came out." He had crawled out and run into the rubber-soled shoes in the hall. Obviously, that never happened again!

At one reunion, Huey Morris told my husband to take good care of me for he really thought a lot of me. He also admitted to me that he had cheated on a test and said how bad I had made him feel when I bragged on him!

Ray Osborn and Marvin Kemp! They were both in my shorthand class and in this class you simply needed to read or write shorthand every night. This was the only course I ever taught that really required homework. Ray usually had his written work, but I was puzzled as to why he could not read his own notes until the day I discovered he was copying Marvin Kemp's work. How did I discover this? In copying his work, he also copied Marvin's name which Marvin had begun to write in shorthand. He ended his homework with "yours truly, Marvin Kemp" in shorthand. That incident followed Ray the rest of the year.

Ned and Ted Brunson were the first twins I had ever known and it was quite interesting to have them in my class and to get to know them.

Sammie Davis and I could have never imagined that in later years, we would sit by the swimming pool and "chat" as our children took swimming lessons.

On workbook pages where students had to fill in their names and the date, Archie Cumpton never failed to put in the "date" blank: "How about Friday night?" At one reunion, when he found out I was there and was now Mrs. W.A. "Bo" Lusk, he strode across the room announcing very loudly as he gave me a big hug, "Bo Lusk, I didn't know you married my *teach!*" I was not aware that they knew each other.

At another reunion, I got the feeling that Marvin Bryant just simply could not remember me, but he has given me a warm welcome at subsequent ones.

Claydeen Clack, a first cousin I had grown up with, did not give me one minute's trouble and he could have. I'll always be grateful to him.

I'm sure there were many others, but these "pals" come to mind: The Lucky Three (Lois Frith, Myristine McNease and Betty Stoecker); James Abrams and Lindsey Wells; Markaye Cooper and Nancy Hunt; Lee Roy Perkins and Joe "Buck" Boles; Anna Mae Nance and Dena Fay Newsom.

Lilwin Newsom gave her time and talents to the Rayville Guest House (among many other causes, I'm sure) where my mother spent almost six years. I will always be grateful to her for the kindness and attention she showed my mother. Mother dearly loved her!

Frank Vineyard has always given me special attention when I visit his and Audie's Flower Shop.

I honestly can't remember this incident, but obviously my students do. It has been mentioned at the last couple of reunions. "Remember the day we had the potato fight?" I was asked. Maybe I am in denial but I can't remember this incident at all. How did they get the potatoes? Obviously, Ray Osborn and W.C. Stockton, among others, remember!

Another incident that I was reminded of was the day the boys jumped out of the window. I have no recall of this incident, either, or who the culprits were. I'm glad it happened on the first floor as it was quite a jump even from this floor!

In fact, all of you from the classes of 1947 and 1948 have been really nice to me and I do enjoy seeing each of you. I did and still do appreciate the many kind gestures you have shown me.

Several reunions have been held to which all former teachers were invited. At the last one, their 45th, held in 1992, someone remarked about twenty minutes into the program that they were all in their 60s and of course, I was still in my 60s, so the confessions began. How could it hurt now? Practically all of us were grandparents. Some of the things they told were things of which I had been completely ignorant...or was I? I had learned very quickly to simply ignore some incidents and they tended to go away.

Through the years, many of my former students have lived close by and we have "bumped into each other" on occasion. I have a few who will sometimes visit or write. Years ago, I recall getting a few letters from Huey Morris when he was in the service, and Ned Brunson looked me up when he was working close to Epps. Virginia Crawford and I attended the same concert one night. (You and I both like Billy Joe Royal, don't we?)

It amazes me to think of the many career choices and successes these former students of mine have achieved. I know of several, but to list them would be doing an injustice, for there are so many and I do not know what many of them are doing or where they are. I'll just bet I would be awfully proud of *almost* all of you.

CONFESSIONS...BY CHRIS
(My Memoirs)

As I was only 19 when I started teaching juniors and seniors in high school (some of whom I believe were my own age or older), I put a self-imposed rule upon myself. I thought it would be wise to never date someone I was teaching. Remember, it was the war years and a few came back to finish high school when discharged.

I received my first check when I was 20 years old, and have never missed a month yet. I should be rich—but I'm not. Only rich in memories! God gives us memories so we might have roses in December.

I had a persistent boyfriend, who will remain nameless, whose habit of having fresh flowers delivered to the school was helpful to me. I regret that I was never serious about him as he surely spent a lot of money on flowers.

I sometimes wore a red dress that everyone seemed to like. I was also bothered with an allergy. Once in the school paper, *The Hornet's Buzz,* a poem appeared about all the teachers. I remember the part about me:

And next through the door, as you can guess

8

Came Miss Clack in that pretty red dress
Loaded down with books and boxes of kleenex

I did not own a car in the beginning and rode my Dad's school bus to and from school. There were times when I needed to stay for a faculty meeting, a party, etc. Two teacher friends were so nice to me. Eunice Jackson, who lived in Rayville, and Eunice Dunn, who lived in Monroe, always invited me to their homes. They were really good friends and I still value the friendship they extended to me. The other teachers on the faculty had taught me and all were very nice to me, but I was much more comfortable with my new friends. Just human nature, I suppose!

I have already given the class of 1947 much credit for my becoming a teacher. After doing the research on that year and discovering that I had 180 students, 90 in four periods of typing, 24 in bookkeeping, and the infamous study hall, I must have loved working with teenagers. I guess teaching was truly my forte!

I actually took my student's grades seriously, probably more so than many of them. It really hurt to have to give anyone a bad grade, especially an F. I somehow felt that *I* was the one who had failed.

The 1947 year of teaching forever etched on my memory a dislike for study halls. It was on the second floor, had two doors opening into the hall and five desks across, with each row seating 17 students. I had 66 last-period students, some of whom I did not teach and did not know too well. I was only 19 years of age and very inexperienced. Needless to say, I shall never forget this last-period study hall!

In 1947 and 1948, the Parish Supervisor was Miss Blanche Miller. She came to visit me, but admitted that she didn't know anything about teaching my subjects. She did, however, offer to help in any way she could. That taught me a valuable lesson really early, for I never dreaded having a supervisor visit me through the years. I just always assumed that I knew as much or more about what I was doing or trying to do than they did, despite their position.

One of the most unique written excuses for missing school was, "Please excuse _____, as Cow Bayou is up." I did not know then, nor do I know now, where this place is located.

I was a child of the Great Depression, as were all of my friends. We did not realize the luxuries we were missing. I recently read a fun definition of the Great Depression. A girl said, "Because there were no malls, everyone was depressed." Believe it or not, I've picked cotton. I did not have to (and didn't when the leaves had worms on them). I joined my cousins because my dad always hired "field hands" and he would not allow me to work along with them. I recall using my cotton-picking money and ordering fabric from the Sears and Roebuck catalog for 10 cents a yard. I was so proud to say that I bought my own dresses. Of course, my mother actually made the dresses. We ate well, with plenty of fresh and canned vegetables. No one could beat my dad smoking cured hams. He always had his "smokehouse" full. Some of my classmates wore dresses made from flowered or printed flour sacks. Luckily, I never did.

I also received most of my education studying by lamplight. Again, I was fortunate as my parents had what was called an "aladdin" lamp. It used oil also, but gave a much brighter light than the ordinary oil lamp.

Another thing I recall as a little girl was waiting for the ice truck to run. This occurred before electricity came to rural northeast Louisiana. How could you enjoy fried chicken, homemade rolls, butterbeans, mashed potatoes and gravy, fried okra and fresh sliced tomatoes without a cold glass of tea? One of my most treasured memories is hearing the tinkling of ice in the glass of tea. I suppose that is why, even today, I keep a pitcher of water with ice in my refrigerator all year long.

When I reflect on my life as a child, I have nothing but happy memories. A friend gave me a key chain that simply says, "You've come a long way, baby." No, I have never smoked, nor do I advocate smoking, but I still have this on my keys today. It has a different meaning for me. Yes, time does change all things.

I've been invited to several reunions of the two classes I

taught at Rayville. One time I attended a tea at Louise Rainer's home. My husband could not attend so my mother went with me. We really dressed up for the occasion. I had on a pretty bright turquoise dress. Imagine my "red face" when viewing pictures someone had brought of a previous reunion. Yes, you guessed it, I had on the same dress. My only comment was, "You know, turquoise has always been a favorite color of mine."

Recently, at a 50th class reunion celebration, I was asked by a good-looking, distinguished ex-student of 67 or 68 years of age what I would have said had he asked me for a date many years ago. He said, "Two of us just never got up the nerve to ask you, but what would you have said? Would you have dated either of us?" Without hesitation, I replied, "Probably!" You must remember that I had decided it would not be wise to date a student, but after fifty years, my answer contradicted this statement. He also asked, "Who would the other student have been?" That student was not in attendance, but believe it or not, I guessed his name! This surely put a 71-year-old on Cloud 9 for several days. I *love* these reunions! (Be sure to read "Confessions…by Chris" in the Epps portion of this book. Sometimes, my thoughts and memories overlap and refer to my entire career.)

I understand when one's memory draws a blank. Sometimes I wonder: did I go to school with this person or did I teach him/her? I have news for you: as times goes by, this condition does not improve. I've recently learned a new word for it: you're having a "microfog." The memory will return eventually. I'm not even sure if this word is in the dictionary or not, but I love it! I must love it because I have microfogs quite often!

One year, Ellie Morgan and I double dated a couple of times and neither of us can remember our dates' names. And that was even before microfog set in.

SUCCESS IN ST. JOSEPH
(1949)

Joseph Moore Davidson

JMD WARRIORS
(formerly Blue Devils)
Colors: Blue and White

"Success is a journey, not a destination."

PRESTIGIOUS PRINCIPAL
Mr. Walter Loren Enete

Mr. Enete was an easy-going, friendly man who maintained discipline and had a very cooperative faculty and student body. It was a pleasure to be a member of his faculty. He had such a unique sense of humor that everyone loved him!

INTRIGUING INFORMATION AND INCIDENTAL INCIDENTS
(Reminiscing)

In 1949, I had only 50 students in all of my classes at JMD.

And then there was the "Rainy Day Schedule." Yes, each day it rained, we got out at 1:00 pm. I really never did know why, but I loved it. After having taught at Rayville with such large classes, I actually thought I was playing.

Charles Redditt, whose mother was a home economics teacher, loved to cook. He was always bringing me and my friend, Gene Tomlin, some sort of "goodies" that he had baked.

Arnold Walker and Daniel Walker found out that my dad loved to hunt. They extended him an invitation to come and hunt with their father. This occurred many times and our dads became good friends. I really appreciated this, because St. Joseph was a hunter's paradise at that time.

Kenneth Clower literally "passed out" in my class one day. I really panicked, but the rest of the students were taking it very calmly. They knew what was happening as he had done it before. He knew how to hold his breath to a count of 10, and then blow hard with his thumb in his mouth so that he would actually pass out for a minute or two. I've seen Kenneth the last few years and we did a lot of reminiscing about school and, of course, about this incident. He still finds it funny!

In later years, Troyce Guice ran for some political office. I remembered him as a shorthand and bookkeeping student and also for his charming personality. I naturally voted for him because I knew he could charm his way to the top if he wished.

I only had four boys in bookkeeping: Allen James, Troyce

15

Guice, Milton Matthews and Mickey Thomas. I thought I was in for a hard time, but believe it or not, we had a good class and I enjoyed it.

In shorthand, I only had three students: Sally Gerbish Troyce Guice, and Willard Jones. Hard to believe, isn't it?

All the students were good to me, but I especially remember the nice things Kay Lynch, Patsy Roberson, Ann Osborn, Charles Redditt, and Ann Rives did for me.

Students who made "A" for a semester are listed below. If an asterisk follows a name, he or she made an A both semesters.

In bookkeeping, Milton Matthews. In general business, Loren Enete, Wanda Jean Gipson, Kay Lynch, * Patsy Roberson * and William Wade Watson.* In Louisiana history, Joann Duncan, Jack Keahey, Ann Osborn* and Charles Redditt.* In shorthand, Sally Gerbish. In typing, Martha Jean Allen,* Venson Lowery, * Garland Melville* and John Swendiz.

CONFESSIONS...by CHRIS
(My Memoirs)

I loved St. Joseph! There were three single teachers on the faculty. Gene Tomlin and I shared an apartment and our other friend was Marge Allen, who lived on the island outside of St. Joe. Many times we took trips together or drove to Natchez or Vicksburg to have dinner.

We stayed at Marge's home frequently. Her mother, Mrs. Bruce Bufkin, was so sweet to us. She did not care how late we stayed out on Saturday night, but insisted that we go to church on Sunday. The maid always woke us and came upstairs with our breakfast. Yes, we were served breakfast in bed!

All the people of St. Joseph were so friendly and eager to make newcomers feel at home. We were invited to parties, teas and socials.

Our principal even *insisted* that we have a good time. If we did not look tired on Monday morning, he would exclaim that he would try to find us some boyfriends.

One of my "off subjects," not in the field of business, was Louisiana history. I'm still amazed at some of my French

16

pronunciations. I know my Cajun friends of the last few years, Bo's army buddies and their wives, will understand. You see, they still haven't taught me how to say *Laissez les bon temps roulez!*

There were several stores in St. Joe of which I have fond memories. I can't remember the name of the dress shop, but we used to love to shop and buy there occasionally. We also liked the café Emilee's where they served *good* food!

Another unique place was where the weekly movie was held on Sunday nights. After church, we attended the movie where we entered with lights on and took our seats. Everyone visited until all the ones who normally came were there, then lights went out, and the movie started.

Once after payday, Marge, Gene and I went to Monroe shopping. We each bought a suit and decided that we needed to go somewhere. We started out to Marshall, Texas (we had heard there were a lot of guys there) but somehow we ended up in Arkansas at the home of Gene's parents. Marge called her mother to report in so she would not be concerned. Yes, we three really had many good times. Marge and I attended summer school at LSU for several summers and double dated a lot. She met and married her husband during one of those summers. I almost did the same, but he will remain nameless!

EFFORTS AT EPPS
(1950-1979)

Epps High School

EHS Panthers
Colors: Black and Gold

"Some people dream of worthy accomplishments, while others stay awake and do them."

HISTORICAL HIGHLIGHTS

My first memory of Epps was the very picturesque old two-story school building. I never dreamed at the time that I would spend twenty-seven of my thirty years of teaching there. In fact, I married a native son, W.A. "Bo" Lusk, and still live in Epps today.

Through the efforts of the late Mr. W.L. Gwin, a school board member, a commerce or business education department was started at Epps in 1950. Through his friendship with my dad, he invited me to apply for the teaching job.

I well remember the first few weeks of school: ten typewriters--and classes were held in the gym until Mr. C.L. Miller could finish his new agricultural department (the present building). My classes and I then moved into what was to be my department for four years. We inherited his old building (which no longer exists) and he left the ear of corn, plow, owl and other plaques on the walls as he had purchased new ones for his building. Thus, my department was aptly called "The Barn."

Someone hooked up a "Walkie-talkie" (I learned recently that C.B. Roberts helped install these) so we could talk with the office without having to walk over there. My room could not be locked. I had no filing cabinet or other much needed equipment and supplies--but we managed.

My department started the first school paper *Panther Tales* and also began the Junior-Senior Banquet tradition, the social highlight of the school year.

I was also the first secretary in the school office, usually for two periods a day. I kept two sets of books, wrote all checks, typed cumulative cards for entering freshmen, the library book order, the principal's correspondence, and did the monthly compiling of all the registers to send to the school board office. Financial reports were filed twice a year for the General Fund and the Athletic Department. It was a lot of work but I enjoyed it. In fact, I volunteered for the job. (Remember my aversion to study halls.)

I was free to get a coke or candy bar and relax when I wished, as long as I kept up with my work. Sometimes I typed tests for my classes and graded papers. I always had students as office help and I came to know them in a way you could not attain by simply having them in a class.

Later in the 1953-54 school year, I was to move into a department in the new high school building. Through the years, my department became one of the better equipped ones in the parish. I always seemed to get what I asked for from Mr. Gwin. He made my years of teaching there most pleasant. Of course, in the years since I retired in 1979, the department has really been updated with computers and electronic equipment.

PRESTIGIOUS PRINCIPALS

Mr. C. W. Gilmore

Mr. Gilmore was a very capable gentleman who became my mentor. He was gentle and kind and maintained discipline in an easy-going manner. He had his own system of filing (everything scattered on his desk) but he could find anything at a moment's notice. He had a built-in computer for a brain and could recollect any date or event.

I thank him for being so patient and understanding when I was a young, inexperienced teacher. His kindness and attitude had a great impact on me and I shall always value his friendship. He was later to become Superintendent of our parish school system.

Mr. J. D. Segars

I enjoyed knowing Mr. Segars and appreciated his compulsion for neatness and filing techniques. He maintained discipline, but many were literally afraid of him. You see, he was never wrong! Someone remarked one time that they could not understand why he bought pencils with erasers on them, but on the other hand, his dogs liked him, so he could not have been all bad!

He was a very versatile person, coached basketball with a passion, liked classical music and grew his own roses, which he delighted in giving to many who were simply awed by him.

Many of us admired how he took really good care of his two girls after the death of his wife.

I thank him for having been a principal dedicated to the things I valued most as a teacher and for his friendship. He retired and became very active in Beta Club work on the state level.

Mr. Donald R. Gwin

I was older than Don. I was out on a maternity leave the year he would have been in my class, so I never knew him as a student. However, we developed a very good rapport with each other. I sincerely felt his method of coping with integration made our school a "safe" one, and I think he deserved much credit for the spirit of cooperation among our faculty and student body.

He kept this verse from the Bible prominently displayed in his office. "When I was a child, I spake as a child, I thought as a child, but when I became a man, I put away childish things." (1 Corinthians 13:11) I never really knew for sure, but I believe he used this verse in disciplining certain students.

I truly want to thank him for renovating my department and for making it possible for me to thoroughly enjoy my last years of teaching. Years after my retirement, Don also retired and became the Parish Superintendent of Schools.

INTRIGUING INFORMATION AND INCIDENTAL INCIDENTS
(Reminiscing)

Truly, how is it possible to recall, in chronological order, the many incidents that just naturally happen in a classroom setting over a span of 27 years? I plan to let my memory tell my story. No, this is in no way an autobiography, just my memories, impressions and perceptions of these phases in my teaching career.

I've already discovered that you, the student, will not always remember the incidents I might tell about you. Since talking to some former students after beginning my book, many do recall the same incident, yet others do not. My plans are to write what simply "pops" into my mind with no thought of which year it might have happened. Dorothy Durgin, a resident of Brooklyn, N.Y., said in writing her memoirs, "I remember a lot more than I thought I would, with one memory triggering another, like threading beads on a string."

I got to truly know many of the juniors of 1950. Their register was the first I had ever kept in my teaching career. For those of you who may not know about a class register, it involved keeping all grades, absentees, and making out report cards. Just a lot of work! This 1951 class and I published the first paper at Epps High School and we also started the Junior Senior Banquet tradition.

Believe it or not, I still have a copy of this first school paper. The students had to cut a stencil and then "ink" the old mimeograph machine to run off copies. A rather messy job, remember? From this small beginning traditionally the senior class would publish the paper the first semester of school and then the junior class would take over after learning the typewriter keyboard. We repeated this cycle each year.

Remember the singing trio of boys in this class? One only had to ask Ray Hemphill, Sam Crawford and Fred Wilson and they would burst into song. They were good! Many recesses and lunch hours were spent listening to these guys sing. Ray Hemphill left Epps and ended up in Hollywood. He had several small parts in movies which we all eagerly anticipated and watched. From West Carroll Parish to Hollywood is a long jump. Ray sent me a "glamour shot," of which I'm proud, and he wrote to me several times. He visited me on a few occasions, and I believe he is now teaching English in California.

Fred Wilson married Evelyn Beasley, became a Baptist minister, and returned from Alabama to be our guest speaker for the Diamond Celebration at our church. We were all *so* proud of him!

Sam Crawford lives in West Monroe, Louisiana, and sings in the choir at the First Baptist Church of West Monroe, the largest Baptist church in our state.

Sybil Ann Gilmore and Billy Leach were high school

24

sweethearts who married and are now grandparents. I get to see them occasionally as their parents still live here.

Marcie Kitchens and I have remained good friends through the years. One of her sons, Mickey, was a friend to our two boys and just became another son to us. Marcie and I sponsored or were Den Mothers to Epps' first Cub Scout Pack 89, in 1969 and 1970. Epps had previously had Boy Scouts, but this was the first Cub Scout Troop. (By the way, Marcie is the same size she was in high school and she's the mother of four! Isn't it disgusting?)

We entered a parish Jamboree and won first place on the skit our Cubs entered in the talent division.

Two of our Cub Scouts are now pastors and the Cub Scout Master, Donnie Linson, is also in the ministry. His brother, Lawrence, or "Tiddler" as he was fondly called, and my son Daryl are our two Cub Scouts in ministerial work. This is outstanding and Marcie and I do not take any credit.

If UFOs really exist, we saw one at a Cub Pack meeting one night. We were just leaving and this huge bright light was passing by below treetop level. It surely gave all of us a strange eerie feeling. I'll just bet all of our Cub Scouts remember. As far as I know, no one else saw it that night. And no, the punch was not spiked!

I used to go to all the ballgames and have actually been known to stand up and holler. My sons simply cannot believe it!

Dolores Carter, Fay Miller and I used to attend some of the parties the classes held.

Once I invited students I had previously taught at Rayville, St. Joseph and Epps to my home for a cookout and party.

Remember my self-imposed rule about dating students? It was still in effect.

At one time smoking (legal smoking) was allowed on campus, under the tree in front of the Agriculture Building. Of course it became known as the Smoking Tree.

Donald Day was a very polite and, I thought, good-looking guy. He always reminded me of Charlie Pride. I never told Donald and I don't know if he sings.

Ag boys used to really know parliamentary procedure. Sometimes in a class meeting, they could get their way by using this to their advantage. Boy, were they proud of themselves, as well they should have been, even though they were "sneaky" about it. Finally the girls learned to be a bit more careful.

I recall having to send the class president, Jimmy Coleman, out of a class meeting. I can't remember the reason now.

I could always tell when Rusty Kitchens was not telling me the truth. When a grown boy says he needs to go to the bathroom, I ask you what is a teacher to do? I usually let him go, knowing full well that he only wanted to get in line for the lunchroom. I was hoping he would get caught, but to the best of my knowledge, he never did.

To Ruth Kitchens I will always be grateful. She used her nursing skills and showed great compassion to my mother while she was in the Rayville Guest House.

A journalism class was added to the curriculum in 1974 and 1975. We published both the school yearbook and the school newspaper. The students thought they would breeze by and have it easy when they discovered that we would use no textbook. I found I was the one who really had to work preparing lectures, projects, etc. I think we all enjoyed these classes. I know I did.

Did you know we have a celebrity among us? If not, check each issue of the parish paper, *The West Carroll Gazette,* under the basketball news. This column is written by none other than Kathy Ratliff, one of our journalism students.

Glenda Thrower and Sita Young, former students, became business teachers and sent me copies of their school papers.

When I first married into the family, David Jones called me "that pretty lady" and still does to this day.

Some things you ignore, remember? Mike Jones gave me a "pat on the rear" when I was leaning over a student's desk and helping with a bookkeeping problem.

Lewis Martin was a good friend of our boys and visited in our home quite often. Before our boys were in braces, Lewis came home with them from church one day, changed into a pair of their jeans, and stayed the evening. The next day when I was washing clothes, as mothers of boys will do, I checked the pockets and found the strangest looking object. I thought "What are they putting in Crackerjacks now?" and threw it away. Later

26

Lewis' mother called to see if I had found his retainer. After she explained what it looked like, I retrieved if from the trash, which luckily we had not burned.

Daryl, my son, came home to lunch each day of his senior year and usually brought a friend or two. That was in 1977, the year I took a sabbatical. (I needed to recharge my batteries.) Andy Johnston and Gerald Talley were the good friends.

In all my years of teaching, I never spanked a student, though I sent a few out or to the office. I worked with juniors and seniors mostly and, of course, they had outgrown spanking. Discipline was of a different sort.

I got married in 1952 and became *Mrs.* Lusk. But, you know, to the students I became not Mrs. Lusk but Miss Lusk. I've noticed through the years that all teachers were called "Miss."

Former students with whom I taught were Jessie Lee Hillman, Pat Butts, Francine Corley, James Kitchens, Glenda Prine, Johnny Simms, Judy Simms, Murrell Brock and Dwain Tharpe.

We had to use fans, but today they have air conditioned the school. The windows are all boarded up and you cannot see out at all. I don't think I would have liked that.

Beverly Monroe remembers my black and white shoes. They had nothing to do with integration, but I think she thought so. I just had this thing about shoes (almost another Imelda Marcos). I still love shoes of various kinds today.

I kept a file of actual business letters to use as examples when introducing the unit on business letters. It was a good teaching tool. Many letters received had errors of placement or misspelled words. My students were made more aware of what was acceptable. In my General Business class, one project I assigned the students was to gather material for a report on some career. I recall Don Lockard ordered material on the FBI and had received a letter from J. Edgar Hoover. It was in my file of business letters. When I retired, I realized that his personal signature was now a collector's item. Instead of throwing it away when I cleaned out my file, I mailed it to Don. He is a successful realtor and appraiser located in Rayville. He tells me he has this letter framed and hanging in his office.

I also collected the artistic work we did in typing preceding the Christmas holidays. Each year, I would show samples to the class and then gather their work for the next classes. I had a folder *full* of this artistic work. I simply could not throw it away, as some of it was twenty years old or older. I don't recall when I first ordered the film on Artistic Typing and got my classes interested. I did not know if my former students would appreciate such a trivial thing, but I managed to return most of the artwork to them. The results let me know that I did the right thing! Many wrote or called to thank me. Don Raley's girls called to ask, "Did my daddy really do that?" One mother told me that she had one for each of her four children and had framed them. That let me know that the work required to return them was worth the effort.

Office helpers and I always had a deposit ready for Mr. Willie Young, our beloved janitor, to take to the bank. He told me that he always knew my deposit from others because I tied a bow-knot with the strings attached to the bag. I never realized that I did that until he told me so.

Mary Margaret Davis lived with her very proper and elegant aunt. Once she got in the habit of eating candy in a very small shorthand class. This really did not disturb anyone, but one day I thought I had better talk to her about it. I said, "I really don't mind your eating the candy, but it's not polite not to share with the whole class." I went on, "And you know one should always brush one's teeth after eating candy." I should have known: the next day she brought us each a candy bar and carefully put her toothbrush and toothpaste on her desk. We all had a big laugh, enjoyed our candy bars, and that was the end of that. Her aunt never knew!

One year, during the period before lunch, Jan Gowan worked in the office with me. She never failed to call home to see what they were having for lunch and she always ended her conversation with "and fix me some French fries." I've often wondered if Jan still likes French fries.

I had the very best duty partner for many years, Mr. C.L.

28

Miller (or just simply "Miller" as he was fondly called). He taught Agriculture and was loved and admired by all. My husband, who has traveled extensively, some of it when he was in World War II, says the trip that still highlights all others was when Miller took the FFA boys on a summer tour and they climbed Pikes Peak in Colorado.

The first second-generation student to teach was Connie Hale, daughter of Yvonne Coates. There were many others, but she was the first.

Supervisors I recall were Mr. H.M. Thomas, Mr. L.H. Willis, Mr. J.L. McKinzie, and Mr. Quitman W. Durbin. For a couple of years when Mr. Donald R. Gwin was principal, the school board required the principal to supervise.

I always received a beautiful corsage, sometimes an orchid, for each of the banquets I sponsored.

I was hoping Janice Prine LaBatt would inherit my department. At that time, the colleges required those pursuing a teaching career to attend a classroom for several days to observe. She had been a former student of mine, she was pretty and she had a good personality. I just knew she would relate to teenagers well. I was truly flattered when she chose to observe me. For some reason, she was not hired and I've always regretted it. I feel that it was our loss.

I had a student in General Business who gave me a real compliment. Carl Adams said, "Mrs. Lusk, this is not my favorite class, but I give you credit for always grading fairly." I always strove to do just that. Carl played the guitar and left Epps for Nashville where he got to know Chet Atkins. He must have had great potential. I've been told that upon Carl's untimely death, Chet Atkins actually attended the funeral.

After Sonny Felker took Typing I, he used to come in my room during one of my classes and grade papers for me. I, of course, asked the students if they minded if I let Sonny grade some of their typing papers. It was fine with them, but later on the only comment was, "Sonny never misses an error and sometimes you do, Mrs. Lusk."

I had one student, Doretha Gray, who brought me her paper and showed me an error I had missed. This did not happen too

29

often. For her honesty, I did not change her grade as it would have brought her grade down a whole letter. I admired her for her honesty.

In one issue of the *Panther Tales,* they called Don Raley the "idiot" of the junior class. Who else went to a ballgame without his ball suit or took a speed test without any paper in his machine? I was to learn years later that Don deliberately messed up on speed tests so I would let Paul Mercer give him a test or two in the back of the room. He said, "After I typed a line or two, I would tell Paul to start the stopwatch." But I'm so proud of Don! With no college education, he has become a very successful business man in our community. His offer of a job is the only one I truly regret not accepting. I've been known to say, "I'll bet he could own half of Epps if he wanted to."

Very sincere and grateful thanks go to Clyde Yates and Donald Lockard. They will know the reason.

Mr. Young and Mr. Polk were janitors for several years. They always kept up with their work. Mr. Young got up each cold morning and turned on all the heaters so our rooms would be warm. A few times when someone might be looking for them, we discovered they could be found in the bookroom playing checkers.

Speaking of the heaters in the classroom, I used mine for a rather unique purpose. I got on a barbecue sandwich binge and soon discovered that I could wrap the bun in foil, put it on the steam heat about thirty minutes before the lunch hour, and have a ready-to-eat sandwich when my hall duty began.

I was told by Yvonne Coates that a group of us stopped by my mom's house one night and that she served us hot chocolate. This is one incident that I had forgotten.

In 1973, I gave assigned seating to an English 8 class. This was the first and only time I ever did this. They must have pushed me to the edge, but I can't remember how.

During a typing class in 1976, Patriska Pearson literally passed out. The boys took her to the office for me and she had to be rushed to the hospital. We discovered that she was diabetic. It had been rumored that she was taking drugs, as sometimes she had to go to the bathroom and take a shot of insulin. This particular day all she needed was a candy bar, but she did not ask for one and went into a diabetic coma. She was ill for several days. We all wrote letters and sent cards and finally she returned to class. I said, "Why didn't you tell us?" She said, "Mrs. Lusk, if I had asked to go get a candy bar, would you have let me?" Not knowing she was diabetic, I'm sure the answer would have been no.

In 1976-77, Larry Lusk was the first EHS student to join the Louisiana High School Rodeo Association and enter rodeos. Glynn Hale was to follow and, to my knowledge, they were the only two.

Jan Gowan entered the rodeo in the capacity of a queen. Most rodeo queens are selected by three basic criteria: appearance, personality and horsemanship. All three are integral to the success of the queen. She did not represent our school, but won Miss Louisiana Rodeo Queen, which earned her the trip to Miss USA Rodeo Queen in Oklahoma City. Of course we were all so proud of her.

We teachers always were assigned hall or playground duty. Other various and sundry jobs were assigned from time to time. For several years, we were required to sell tickets at the entrance of the gym for ballgames. This was the only job I ever really dreaded. This was before computers and when a spectator asked for tickets for three adults and four children, you had to calculate in your head and make proper change. Sometimes I literally "drew a blank," especially when someone wanted two wholes and five halves. The prices were different for adults, children and school students. I use this means to apologize to any whom I might have short-changed. After a night of this, I truly felt that I had earned my money for the day.

For many years, it was traditional to take the juniors and seniors on a picnic for the end-of-school activities. We either went to Lake Providence, Louisiana, or Vicksburg, Mississippi. I really got my quota of these trips. I would like to say that the students were always on their best behavior.

Mary Margaret Davis and Sue Shows *loved* Elvis and his music--so much so that when he died I sent Mary Margaret a sympathy card. Not really too nice of me! I was simply getting her back for a few of the stunts she had pulled on me. We had a student, Larry Hale, who really was better looking than Elvis in my opinion. He played guitar and imitated him. Marsha Neal, in grammar school at the time, thought he really was Elvis. As kids will do to show off, she turned cartwheels. She truly thought for a long time that he was really *the* Elvis Presley.

I had seen Malcolm Butler on several occasions, but at the last reunion he had put on a little weight (haven't most of us?) Because his hair was so different (he wore bangs), it completely threw me off for a while. I found the voice and smile so familiar, but it took me a while to put a name with the face. I really think I hurt his feelings. I'm sure he was thinking. "How can she forget one of her favorite pests?"

Paul Mercer was another favorite "pest" of mine whom I did not recognize, but I had not seen him in years. To me, he still does not look at all like the Paul of the old high school days. Actually, I would not have recognized him had I met him on the street!

Charles E. Pruitt won the art contest for the logo on the cover of the school paper *Panther Tales*. It was a panther whose long tail wrote Panther Tales. I was also told he invented an electric mouse trap.

In all my 30 years of teaching, I had only one student who ever questioned me about a grade. Believe it or not, it was sweet li'l ole Clyde Yates. He had transferred here from Delhi, Louisiana, and they sent his actual grade instead of a letter grade. Our scale for grades was higher than their scale so his average was lowered. After checking with the principal, we got it all straightened out to everyone's satisfaction.

Students that told jokes and were witty (the ones that I recall): Janice Prine, Larry Lusk, Jimmy Holmes, Marianne Kitchens, Donnie Linson, Barry Cook, Robert Jones, Linda Brown, Pam Lingefelt, Gary Miller, John Mercer, Mary Margaret Davis, Robin Fryer, Jessie Humes, Mark Miller, John Graham, Francine Corley, Jo Ann Humes, Candy Jones, Robertina May, Allen Hendrix.

In 1950 and 1953, I had to teach PE! Would you believe volleyball?

Burlen White was a very distinguished-looking guy. He was the only person I ever knew who had one blue eye and one brown eye.

I had two students who knew origami, the art of folding paper. David Hogan could make a duck with wings that flapped when its tail was pulled. Bonnie Weatherly could make beautiful snowflakes by folding and then cutting the paper. I have one of each.

Pam Hale, who is very active in Cub Scout work, was asked while taking a course to name someone who had influenced her life. She told me that she put down my name. Now that really was a compliment! (Be sure to read the section entitled "Nice Notes." There are several compliments of which I am extremely proud.) You can't help but believe that they are sincere when they have nothing to gain by giving them. What I'm really trying to say is that they can't be considered a bribe!

Fay and Kay Hall were the second set of twins that I had the pleasure of teaching. They were both straight A students. I had a hard time telling them apart, though they were not identical. (Craig Yates was of no help.) My son Daryl always thought they told on him. He would say, "I bet Kay or Fay told you." I usually kept him guessing.

Back when the teacher had permission to excuse a child from class without sending him/her to the office, C. E. Corley pulled the "stomach ache trick" on me. One had only to look at him to tell he was really in pain. He pulled this stunt on me several times before I caught on. I was skeptical, but he was so convincing.

I had a large class of Typing I students one year. I believe I had just introduced the tabulator and how it worked, so was having to give a lot of individual help to the students. Robert Jones, who could not do anything *quietly*, kept calling, "Mrs Lusk, I need you. Please come here." "I will, Robert, as soon as I work my way up to where you are." "But, Mrs. Lusk, I need you now." And again, "Mrs. Lusk, please come here and help me *sot* my margins and I'll type." Yes, Robert, you really did say *sot* and not *set*. He was using a Royal typewriter with the Magic Margin system and the margins were locked, so his typewriter carriage would not move. After showing him what had happened, I set his margins for him. He settled down and quietly typed. Typing was a struggle for Robert in the beginning. He had what I usually called "flying fingers," but he was determined! He got a typewriter at home and I let him check out a typing book. He actually became the very *best* typist I had that year. I was truly proud of you, Robert!

Remember pretty and talented Ann Skipper? She was really good on the piano and she could type too! And who can forget the two sweet Morrow girls, Dianne and Debbie?

My son Daryl and his friend Lewis Martin took piano lessons for several years. When I discovered Daryl hiding his music among other books, I realized I was just wasting my money and let him drop his lessons. I have to brag a bit. His teacher told me she had taught him all she could, that all he needed to do was practice. He could read notes as well as play by ear. The piano teachers I remember are Jo Donald, Maxine Holmes and Vonda Fraley and I believe Sylvia Glidewell also taught piano lessons.

I remember notorious books through the years. When I was in college in the '40s, it was *Forever Amber*, then *Peyton Place*, and before I retired, it was *The Happy Hooker*. I know Chris King will remember! It's hard for me to realize that some books are even worse now and, in my opinion, most TV shows are not suitable for children.

One year my class was selling magazines to make money for a project. Patricia Ezell, the student who sold the most, received a nice prize from the company. Someone said, "Mrs. Lusk, I know why Patricia won, because they bought from her just to get her to shut up!" That's all right, Patricia, you still won!

At a recent reunion, Nelda Leach could not recognize me at all. A classmate said, "Nelda, this is Mrs. Lusk." "Oh yes," she replied, "but Mrs. Lusk did not teach me. I was in Mrs. Whitaker's room." That only aged me about twelve years in an instant. A Mrs. Lusk did teach first grade, but I was the Lusk in high school.

Laney Rhymes told me that my encouragement pushed him to run for a state office in FFA and he won. I was so proud of him because I could tell he possessed the potential.

I had the students in one English class sign their names to a sheet of paper to help me remember their names. Upon looking over the list, I remarked, "OK, who's the wise guy? Who's Sweetpea?" A cute little blonde raised his hand. I asked, "Don't you have a real name?" "Yes," he said, "but everyone calls me Sweetpea." Guess what, I was calling him Sweetpea before the year was over.

The content of the subjects I taught helped many achieve their life's work without pursuing further education (Marianne Kitchens, Ruth Thornton, Sue Black and Donna Duckworth). I'm sure there are others who do not come to mind. I'm especially proud of Julie Nielsen, who is now head bookkeeper for Guaranty Bank in Delhi, Louisiana.

For many years, we did not have a guidance counselor for our school or parish. We teachers more or less counseled our students. I know I've had several come to me to talk, but two stand out above the rest. Loretta Brock and Billie Ruth Crnkovic will tell you today that they wish they had listened to me.

Mike Jones kept talking in class one day and I became so exasperated that I said, "Mike, I hope you take laryngitis tonight so you'll be quiet tomorrow." Believe it or not, *I* had laryngitis the next day and could not talk above a whisper.

Freddy Tannehill would sometimes call me "stuck-up" because I did not wave to him. Quite often I drove to my parents' home after school. Freddy must have lived at least a half mile off the main highway. No way could I see him wave. Oh, that Freddy! He either liked typing or me. He took Typing I and failed and repeated it again the next year and failed again. Would you believe he took Typing I a third time and passed. How did this happen? He was scheduled in a Typing II class and quite often I would fail to assign him new jobs. Naturally, he wasn't going to ask for any new jobs, so he squeezed by. He was never a troublemaker--he just simply could not type!

I had some crackerjack ball players in a bookkeeping class. They had to be separated during tests. I told them their "shifty" eyes were the reason they could fake so well in the ballgame. They were Larry Ball, C. E. Corley, John Mercer, Henry Newton, E. V. Roberts and J. A. Works. I dare any of them to dispute what I've just said!

In 1964, Maxine Gowan, an adult, took Typing I with my regular class. Becky Plunkett also audited several of my classes. She was a *whiz!*

In 1969, Clerical Practice was added to the curriculum for the first time. In 1974, I used a new method of grading (Skill and Production Grading). The grades could be improved by standardized objective tests, not lowered. Points were given on basis of errors made and then converted to a letter grade.

The year Benny Tannehill took shorthand, he developed his own unique shortcut method when taking dictation. When I discovered I could not read his dictation notes, it was almost too late to change him. He was able to read it and type a presentable letter from his notes so I let him continue his own method. We teased him about his "Tannehand" method and he was able to pass the course.

Do any of you recall the several days that Leatrice Calhoun cried all day? I'll bet she can't even remember his name now. Another sad little girl was Wanda Smith, who had a friend called Rose, and they both had a friend called Bud. Need I say more?

On the days we typed to music, it was so hard for Fannie Gray to simply sit and type. She had rhythm all over her. I can hear her now, "But, Mrs. Lusk, it's so hard to just sit here."

In bookkeeping classes, after we were able to afford the 10-key electric adding machine, I told my students not to copy my method. You see, in college we only had the full-key machines and I never really mastered the "touch" on the 10-key. I would show my students the correct touch method. Many were able to learn it, but Wayne Tanner stands out in my memory as *mastering the touch*. He was really fast and accurate.

J. T. Thornton enrolled in my typing class and later dropped it. He told me recently that it was not me, he just did not like typing. He took agriculture instead and became really interested in horticulture. He finished college in Veterinary Science and horticulture has become quite a profitable hobby for him. He cross-pollinates and has had the honor of naming several hybrid plants. He laughed and said, "So I give typing credit for my career choice." He says he still can't type.

I had one other student that I recall who literally hated typing, speed tests and the pressure of getting work in on time. She said even the noise of the typewriters bothered her. Needless to say, the business field was not June Coody's choice; she became a nurse.

None of my subjects were required; all were elective. When someone would gripe or complain about something, I loved to say, "You do not have to take my subject; it is not required and you may leave by either door." My room was large with two doors. Actually, no one ever left.

As I mentioned, my room had two doors. Sometimes during class changes, a student or two would walk through my room instead of the hall. I let them change the paper guide on the typewriter, lock the margins, loosen the cylinder, etc. Of course, the class thought the other classes were doing it. To me, it was a good teaching tool, as it taught the students to check the typewriter before doing a production job.

Sue Black and I decided that we must like each other. One year, she took three of my classes and worked with me in the office the other three periods. She was so sweet and efficient and everyone loved her. We had fun! I must also mention "Suzie" (Dorothy Collins). She and I had fun in the office. Another office worker I simply cannot fail to mention is Janie Carter. She was an information bureau. She knew *everything*. I wish I had a list of all who helped me through the years.

Stevie Miller and Joe Cleveland worked with me in the office one year. They helped me antique the old desk I was using. Mr. Segars bought glass to cover the top of the desk and a secretary chair. Steve and Joe picked out the pattern and covered two cafeteria chairs to go in my office. I made a couple of flower arrangements and it really looked nice. I want Stevie and Joe to know that after I retired, the school was planning on trashing this desk and I luckily retrieved it. I had used it in the office since 1954 and prior to that Mr. Gilmore had used it in the upstairs office in the two-story building (which no longer exists).

In the school year 1962-63, the class photograph was not sold to the students. About four boys were seated on the front row and two of them slipped in an ugly sign. Mr. Segars would not sell the picture to the students. I have one, however, and I know the guilty ones, but I'll not tell. If they read this book, they will remember.

I also know who painted "Yours truly" and a name on the back of the old bank building. I'll not tell. It's written in shorthand so not too many of you can read it.

Halloween used to be a hoot! Traditionally, an old outdoor "John" was placed on the school campus and all the windows were soaped, some with signatures. The next day, they had to wash all the windows and remove the john, but they got out of class to do it. I know the outdoor toilets were used in 1976, because I have a picture of one at the front school entrance. They finally ran out of johns and started "rolling" the shrubs and trees.

I shall always remember Stephanie Waller and her compassionate ways. She helped my "feelings" on several occasions.

One junior class voted to work on a banquet after school. I believe it was the class of 1955 or 1956. I can't remember which.

John White, a former student, became a cop and worked for many years in Oak Grove. He said he couldn't wait to catch an Epps teacher. I'll tell you the truth — I always drove *slowly* when there.

I recall Louie Cleveland, a very good basketball player, who simply could not concentrate on his work just prior to a game. He could see the team arrive out of our windows in the bookkeeping class. He would say, "Mrs. Lusk, just let me sit here quietly and I'll get my work in by Monday." I did and he would hand in his work on time. I really think he was meditating and doing a lot of positive thinking. Apparently, no one in the class knew — but it happened every Friday that we had ball games scheduled.

This incident did not happen in my class, but I just have to include it. Before we had air-conditioning, sometimes it was so sultry hot that the classroom doors had to be opened to create a cross-ventilation. I usually had two fans on, and kept my doors closed so the roar of the typewriters would not interfere with classrooms close to my department.

On this particular day, Gary Miller was taking an American history test, and the voice of Mrs. Gilmore, the math teacher, could be heard distinctly as her room was just across the hall. After the class, he went to his next class in the English room and simply collapsed in his desk. Upon being asked by the teacher, Mrs. Holmes, what was the matter with him, he replied, "I think I just took the square root of Thomas Jefferson."

His mother, Lou Miller, a second grade teacher, related this cute anecdote to me. She was writing on the blackboard and challenged her students to copy what she had written, doing it exactly like she had done. One of her students made a big mess, and she knew he could write better. She reprimanded him, and his reply was, "But, Mrs. Miller, that's the best I could do using my left hand." You see, he was right-handed.

Erline Jones, who taught many of you, related this story to me. I just had to include it. She taught American history, and being very well-read often interjected intriguing intimate details and incidents into her lectures. One such incident was about courting couples during the early days of American history. She told her class that after the embers in the fireplace were low, the couples sometimes simply had to get into bed under the covers to keep warm. But the custom was to use the "chastity board" which reached the entire length of the bed to completely separate the two. Really interesting! One day, a boy asked, "Mrs. Jones, do you suppose there were ever any knotholes in the board?" After laughter subsided, she remarked, "I really don't know!" and continued with her lecture.

I've had various excuses given to me for missing my classes, but two really stand out in my memory. "I'm taking my girlfriend to the doctor to see if she is pregnant" and "I have to attend court for hunting out-of-season." Yes, I know who these people were, but I'm not telling!

One excuse came from Delores Glosson, who was in a Typing II class. I discovered she simply did not know the keyboard. I told her that she was in the wrong class and needed to be enrolled in my Typing I class. She said, "But Mrs. Lusk, I have already had Typing I." So I asked, "But how did you pass?" She looked up at me and remarked, "I was graded mostly on charm and personality." Needless to say, that year she had to repeat Typing I.

I've had various compliments from time to time. Some are simply outstanding. Mickey Black, an adopted son, came into my class one day and remarked, "Mrs. Lusk, you look like a million today" and then added "every year of it."

Recently, Ronald Lingefelt told me something that James Kitchens had remarked. They were both pallbearers at a funeral recently and saw me as I walked up the sidewalk and entered the church. James remarked, "She looks like a tall bottle of pepto-bismol." I was wearing a cherry pink dress. Was that a compliment or not? I'll have to think about that one!

When my typing room was so crowded that two desks had to be side-by-side, I believe a romance got started at the typewriters. At any rate, these two began to date and later got married. Remember Jeff Guice and Pam Lingefelt? Poor Pam, Jeff was always moving her margin or setting the ribbon on stencil typing—anything to mess up her work.

Raymond Lingefelt repeated Typing I for no credit one year. He would occasionally type tests for me and made a little spending money typing term papers for the American history students. I had to encourage him to charge for this. He was willing to do it for free. I also discovered he repeated Shorthand in 1967. Like Freddy Tannehill, I never knew whether Raymond liked me or my subjects—or did I? Raymond was one of my very capable editors of *Panther Tales*.

In one of my English classes, J.E. Alexander handed in the cleverest paper I've ever had on giving directions. He had a country mouse visit his city mouse cousin who lived in the school building. He took him on a grand tour of the buildings and classrooms, explaining them as they went from room to room. I wish I had kept it!

This has nothing to do with teaching, but the above incident reminded me of it. I once had a boyfriend who wanted to become much more involved than I did, and his letters proved it. I wrote him back, saying something to the effect, "If you want to remain friends with me, let's keep it breezy." My next letter from him was about nothing but the wind and the breeze from a tropical isle to the fierce wind of a tornado. It would have made a perfect essay for college. I wish I had kept it. Oh yes, he signed it, "Out of Breath."

I remember P. M. Alexander and Harlan Tanner as very tall boys who could make those long shots in basketball from the center line and score.

One day when my son Larry was FFA president, he waited until last period to mention to me that the club would be meeting at our house that night. He had to go grocery shopping and help me, because the trend at that time was to eat a meal at the house in which the meeting was held. Talk about the urge to kill…but when I found a vase of camellias in my kitchen window, I melted. Yes, he knew how to con his own mother.

I tried to incorporate as much variety as possible into my business classes. We always took a field trip to the State Farm Insurance office located in Monroe. We walked to our local bank after finishing the bookkeeping chapter on banking. I'll just bet the students will remember the ice cream cones I bought them at Malissa's on the way back to school. Would you believe, two scoops for a nickel! I've been told a cup of coffee never sold for more than 5¢ until the day she closed the cafe.

We also had speakers come and talk on various subjects and career choices: bankers from neighboring towns; Harry Addison, a humorist and businessman from Monroe; also a representative of BMI, a Monroe-based business school, and many others. Also, Ruth Boyette, a former student, demonstrated posting machines and talked to the class about banking procedures.

I like to say that we were "country" before "country" was cool. Sounds like Barbara Mandrell, doesn't it? During the years before I moved into my new department in the new high school building, even our typewriter tables were homemade. My bookkeeping class had to move the typewriters over and use the available space that was left. This was very inconvenient because, as bookkeepers know, they need to spread their work in front of them.

During the years, I have had many boys who could repair a typewriter just by comparing it to one of the same make. If I recall, the repair man only came once a six-week period, and then only if needed. There were no routine checks!

There were a few years when we had an "open" campus. Because the "drug scene" was new, most of us adults had a lot to learn. In retrospect, I believe a few times some students in my classes were feeling mighty "good"—or was the expression "high."

My husband and sons included a poolroom in our home. Almost all the younger set in Epps visited and played pool. The rules were: no drinking, no horseplay and no foul language. Only two mishaps happened to my knowledge. The glass was broken on the gun case door, and a hole was found in the acoustic-tiled ceiling, exactly the size of the end of a cue stick. My granddaughters and friends have also shot many games of pool there. Only once was anything missing and that was a cue ball which was never found. I will call no names, but am 99 and 44/100 percent sure I know who the guilty party is. Oh, well, I replaced it!

Dawn Collins told me one day that she met a guy, H.C. Clark, who said I had taught him in Rayville. I remarked, "Oh, yes, I remember H.C. He had reddish blonde hair." She said, "I don't know, Mrs. Lusk, for he is completely bald." That added a few years to my age in a hurry.

One of the best definitions of vocabulary words in bookkeeping was the student who defined an "outstanding check" as one that "stands out."

Linda Hale told me the other day at a reunion that she loved typing, but would get so nervous if she thought I was close by and might be watching her. I'll just bet many others may have felt this same way.

Walter Hillman, I do not mean to embarrass you, but you were the only Hillman I ever taught who was not a straight A student. You made a few B's for me. I think I know the reason. When you were typing, the letters SONJA FOX were uppermost in your mind. Some words required use of other letters of the alphabet. Am I correct? I also thought she was cute!

At a recent reunion of the class of 1958 (their fortieth), once again we teachers received many compliments. I feel that they are sincere as they really have nothing to gain. But on the other hand, after seeing us as we have aged, maybe, just maybe, they were trying to make us feel better. Anyway, it is always fun for me.

At a recent reunion, Sheldon Ezell cooked the delicious meal, even including some of the desserts. His wife is a lucky lady to have a wonderful cook in the family. My Bo doesn't even know how to boil an egg. I must admit, though, that he has perfected his outside grilling. To keep peace, I thought I had better mention that fact.

Sheldon said the reason I always managed to maintain discipline was that he and all the boys thought I was so pretty that they did not want to misbehave and put a frown on my face. Wasn't that a nice compliment! Actually, I believe that my subject matter had a great deal to do with my class discipline. In typing, for the most part, it was a hands-on experience. No boring lectures! Again, very few lectures were required in bookkeeping. All worked on projects, problems, practice sets, adding machines and calculators, which involved the students. In my opinion, a teacher whose class requires a lot of lecturing and notetaking has to be really good to hold the student's attention. Shorthand was a *fun* subject--and one that is no longer taught now that we have all the new technology and machines. I still use my shorthand, especially around Christmas when I want to mark a gift and keep it a secret. My granddaughters say, "Nanny, that's not fair!"

Notice that I'm not commenting on my English classes. Need I say more? For one thing, the students were younger and I preferred to teach the older students.

One year, Buddy Simms and some other boys really "griped" when they had to go to the west swamp and cut some large palmettos. They were to be used to help decorate the stage and the finished project was very pretty. We received several compliments. The boys simply could not conceive of something growing wild in a pasture looking good on the stage.

To tell on myself, I suppose I must include this peculiarity of mine. I truly cannot tell directions and am not completely aware of where I am most of the time. (I mean this in a physical sense, not mental.) I like to say, "I just sometimes take the scenic route," when the actual truth is I get lost easily. I was always afraid my friends and some of the relatives might think I was just trying to get attention. A couple of years ago, my granddaughter Taffy saw a stack of letters tied up with a bow. When she discovered they were old love letters of mine, she simply had to read one. She chose one at random and among other things I had written, "Bo, would you believe in going through Natchez to Baton Rouge, I took the wrong exit and found myself headed to Brookhaven?" Taffy commented, "Nanny, you've been lost all of your life, haven't you?"

I was relating this story to Marcie Kitchens, a former student of mine. She said, "Include that in your book, because I can vouch for the accuracy of it." She remembers when I used to help take ballplayers home after the games and they always had to tell me whether to turn left or right. I was told that they used to laugh behind my back because I never knew which way to go. Sometimes, time *does not* change things!

Wayne McMillan works at a medical lab and each evening must record data on the computer. He tells me he gets to leave before the others because of the typing skills he uses on the computer. He is finished while all the others are still *slowly* typing their data. He remarked, "I'm so glad I took typing."

A skit that stands out in my memory had students enacting a classroom scene in which the class represented all the present teachers on the faculty. As I recall, the student who portrayed the teacher kept calling me down, "Chris," she said, "you sit down, stop talking and start typing." One other class member that I recall was this teacher who was always tying to *cheat*. Now, this did not go over with this particular teacher as you did not do *anything* in her class, epecially cheat. I always wondered where her sense of humor was.

Sonny Fox was really a "ladies' man." He was polite and goodlooking and all the girls in the school had a crush on him.

Toni Newton and Sue Sealy Phillips have always been really good friends. They still keep in touch today. Toni told me recently that she and Sue had lunch together in New Orleans. I believe Sue lives in Alabama.

Believe it or not, we teachers used to stay after school and once we learned to square dance. One time, a few of us actually performed on the stage for a fun time. Our students were simply amazed! You know, in most of their minds, we teachers were not supposed to be "normal" in any sense of the word.

I do not mean to be disrespectful but this next skit is about the late Mr. J. D. Segars. It was so cute and he enjoyed it so much that I do not think it inappropriate to describe it here. One of his classes very cleverly gave him a "mock funeral." The message was delivered from a Sears, Roebuck catalog. The preacher, Fred Wilson (who actually later became a pastor) delivered the eulogy by simply reciting the ABCs with emphasis and pounding on certain letters. His voice inflections were perfect. Each member, dressed rather outlandishly, filed by the makeshift casket. Each, tearfully or otherwise, had some very complimentary things to say about him. Some were truly compliments, some were jokes--anything to poke a little fun. The ending was quite dramatic! A body (Mr. Segars himself) slowly raised from the open casket and apparently had been dreaming! He immediately dispersed the crowd and sent them back to class.

One of my students, Raymond Lingefelt, insisted that I attend his wedding. He was one of my "special" students so I did attend. As far as I know, he has been happily married all these years.

Steve Miller possessed a talent that he did not display too often. I have heard him sing and his voice always reminded me of the famous singer Bobby Vinton.

Three of my favorite beauticians have been former students: Judy Oldham, Fran Payne and Lisa Simms.

ᐱ Robin Black and Annette Runions were "pals" in high school. Both have crossed my path in various ways since those school days. My memories of them are fond.

ᐱ Mitchell Donohue and Byron Boykin are others who are in ministerial work. I'm so proud to hear this about them.

ᐱ Candy Jones, the loud mouth, could be heard all over the school. She said what she thought, but everyone loved her.

ᐱ Julie Jones could get by with almost anything. She only had to give me that cute smile.

ᐱ When you think of Julie Jones and high school, you just naturally think of Andy Johnston. He was another student with personality plus and a winning smile.

ᐱ Lisa Simms, how could I have dreamed back when I taught "Buddy" Simms and Mary Ann Guice that their daughter would one day become my own daughter-in-law and the mother of two of my "special" granddaughters?

ᐱ David Jones teaches school and dabbles in politics. He is now our mayor. His mother, Erline Jones, was mayor pro tem a few years back.

ᐱ Randy Miller, do you remember when we were seated together at an FFA banquet? You kept me giggling and laughing. I was afraid they were going to throw us out!

I recall when I thought I was a good ping-pong player and even bragged about it. Was I surprised and embarrassed when Dwain Tharpe really beat me big time!

ᐱ Dennis LaBatt is one "Yankee transplant" that everyone likes and most are really proud of him. We should be! He is a great PR man for Epps and especially Poverty Point. You may be interested to know that he was married to an Epps girl, Janice Prine, on top of one of the mounds. I also know he loves sunflower seeds. He shares with me when we attend the same ball games. Here comes that *misfit* again! He is watching his daughters and Bo and I are watching our granddaughters play.

Connie Plunkett took typing from me. She had the longest straight dark hair that was so pretty! I simply could not resist the temptation to lift it (it was surprisingly heavy) each time I passed her desk.

✓ Marvin Boyette and Maurice Starks, former students, became my "favorite" electrician and plumber, respectively.

✓ Helen Butts and I have been friends for a long, long time. I value her friendship, and will always remember the nice things she did for my "kids."

✓ With David White's help, we did some landscaping on our church grounds. I think of him quite often when I notice the plants.

Charlie Fryer and a group played music for us at one of our banquets. They were really good!

I remembered Harold Leach as a rather retiring and shy student. At a recent reunion, he displayed personality plus, and is a very busy retired aerospace scientist. Among his many activities, two intrigued me the most. He not only works jigsaw puzzles, but actually makes them for some company. He is also a volunteer weather spotter.

✓ Bennie Roberson remembered the year I was married: 1952. He said, "Mrs, Lusk, you were always planning menus." I certainly did, for I quite often wondered what to prepare for my husband. We shared only one meal together each day. I did not know any of my students were aware of this fact.

C. B. Roberts related this amusing incident. At one time many of the girls were wearing tiny jingle-bells on their shoes or on one of the many crinoline slips that were worn back then. Charles Earl Pruitt came to school one day with a cowbell tied on each leg. Of course the noise was very loud! Mr. Gilmore reprimanded him and he replied, "But, Mr. Gilmore, the girls wear jingle bells and I just wanted to outdo them." (He was tired of hearing the bells.) Needless to say, all bells were banned that day. Many of us were glad.

Several of my ex-students, including C.B. Roberts and wife and Maurice Nelson and husband, belong to AWS (Adults With Seniority). They take trips together, visit each other often and seemingly have a good time. I think it is always rewarding to keep in touch with your friends from the past.

✓ Shirley Aaron gave me the nicest compliment at a recent reunion. It was really worth an A+, but I didn't have my grade book with me. She attended in place of her husband, Bonnie

Simms, a 1953 graduate, who did not get to come. Shirley still looks great.

Neal Clack, a relative and former student, has become a self-made man. I'm so proud of him. He is the service officer for the Veterans Affairs office in our parish of West Carroll and also in Morehouse parish.

Both Neal Clack and Mickey Black were former students who served in the Desert Storm Gulf War. I had their addresses and wrote to them a few times during that period.

An ex-student recently told, Bo, "I thought Mrs. Lusk was so pretty. I couldn't wait to get in her classes, but I failed and never did make it to high school." I didn't know you cared, John Earl (Johnny).

Don and Gary Neal Crouch lived on my street and both were in my classes. We were related as our grandfathers were brothers. From time to time, Don would help me in my yard. Soon after building our new home, I can still hear Don's comment: "Mrs Lusk, you have the prettiest bathroom on the block."

Steve Hillman and Gene Hale! I never had the pleasure of teaching them, but they visited me quite often in the office.

I shall never forget the "breaking news" Don Crouch related to me in the parking lot as I arrived for school one morning. I'm sure Don remembers too.

I wish to mention Kim Hale in a special way. She was quiet, sweet and efficient, as were Pam Oliphant, Connie Gwin, Anis and Mary Martin.

An incident of historical importance happened to my grandfather, Dave Williams, who was shot by his friend, Bob Oldham. The story goes that it was a dispute over some hogs. As my grandfather went to shake Bob's hand, Bob thought he had gone for his gun and shot him. I was told that Bob said, "What have I done? I've killed my best friend." Possibly a very unique situation happened because of this incident. As a teacher, I taught descendants of the man who had killed my grandfather. We simply laughed about the matter. Our forefathers were involved in this incident, not us! I've never really grasped the

48

reason some groups blame others for things that happened years ago when they themselves were not actually involved.

I've been told that the last year I taught, Doug Ed Fairchild intentionally tried my patience to get me to break my record. I really don't remember this incident, but was told that I said something to this effect, "Doug Ed, I don't care what you do or say, I'm not going to break my record and spank you!" They said that once he realized that I simply was not going to spank him, he settled down and behaved.

At a recent funeral, someone approached me from the back and said, "Hello, good-looking! Guess who's hugging you!" I turned to see a pair of twinkling eyes and a ready smile partially hidden by a mustache. He was a very handsome guy! Even though in 30 years, he had added a little weight and a few gray strands at the temples, I recognized him. We had a short visit and that afternoon he came to my home for a visit. He was quite interested in the idea of my book. He said that after all these years, he wanted to confess something to me. "I've loved you since the ninth grade and, after seeing you today, I still do." I was simply flabbergasted!

He continued, "Bo is surely a lucky man. And you may put this in your book and use my name!" Needless to say, I've been on Cloud 9 for several days. No, there was never any hanky-panky. In retrospect, I do recall that more than being a favorite pest, he was somehow always very special to me. And yes, for intrigue, he will remain nameless!

RIGHT OR WRONG...I DID IT "MY WAY"

It seemed to work for me. As I have previously stated, Mr. W.L. Gwin always tried to fill my requests for supplies and equipment. In the school year 1954-55, Gregg Publishing Company had available a series of typewriting rhythm records ranging in speed from 16 to 52 words per minute. I purchased this set and a record player. I was also able to purchase dictation records for shorthand and slides for use with an overhead projector for any bookkeeping classes.

After a series of jobs was completed, I would emphasize

speed. By using these records, which had a definite beat with a classical music background, my students were able to push their speed levels higher. Many times we had a contest between the classes, basing the winners on speed. There were a few classes with vacant typewriters and I would sometimes take speed tests with the classes, until Ronnie Corley and Phil Jackson could both beat me. After that I always found some excuse not to take speed tests with them.

As I recall, many of the students loved this "sprint for speed." Others simply hated it, and some did not like the music on the Rhythm Records.

I always tried to create a business or office atmosphere in my room, especially the typing, clerical practice and shorthand classes. My students were free to go to the filing cabinet, my desk or a table where the paper cutter, stapler and hole-puncher were kept without getting permission from me. I also did not mind if they stopped and looked at a job another student was working on, provided they did not disturb the class.

The first year after acquiring the record player, I brought Christmas music from home to play in the background, since no new jobs were introduced just prior to the holidays. In fact, we started a tradition of artistic work on the typewriter. Yes, one can actually create pictures by using various keys in different ways. I had a set of books with instructions, but many students started branching out on their own and created some very unique designs. I must say, I got my best work from J. E. Miller at this time. His was a huge "Clyde the Camel," complete with sequins and glitter. I don't mean to offend you, J. E., but you know this is true.

Many will remember the Christmas music by Andre Kostelanetz, Elvis Presley, Perry Como, Andy Williams and a "Treasury of Christmas" by a host of popular and classical artists. I've always loved music, and after Christmas when the introduction of a new unit was thoroughly covered, we settled down to actually doing the production work. I thought I would broaden their appreciation of music by continuing to use soft background music. I introduced them to the Longines Symphonette Society with "The Treasury of the Golden West," including all songs of our American heritage. This was accepted very well and the students were well-behaved. Possibly you can guess the rest. After a new unit was introduced and production work was begun, more music! We covered the entire spectrum of music. They were free to bring records of their own with my approval. We went from Hawaiian to country, to popular and classical--even to some rock and roll.

I connect certain music with various students. I remember Ronnie Powell's love of Hugo Montenegro, Marsha Neal who liked Johnny Rivers, and Mary Margaret Davis and Sue Shows who preferred Elvis. Paul Mercer introduced me to Johnny Horton. Joe Gilmore told me recently that he always thought of me and typing class when he heard a song by The Platters. And then there were Engelbert Humperdinck, Tom Jones, Ray Anthony, and the list goes on and on.

BETA CLUB CONVENTIONS

Erline Jones and I took the students to many Beta Club Conventions held in Baton Rouge. It was fun and we did not ever have any serious problems. Once I woke up with a fever and sore throat, and could not find anyone to go in my place. I called the doctor, he gave me a shot and some antibiotics, and I made the trip to keep them from being disappointed. Erline's children, as well as my son Daryl, were members of this honorary club.

Erline and I loved these trips because we got to shop at a big discount store. We found many bargains. Usually, we bought formal dresses for the last night—the night of the big banquet.

APPLES FOR THE TEACHER

No, I never received an apple in the traditional sense. Before we had filing cabinets, the students had to come to my desk for paper, carbons, etc. One particular day I had brought an apple to school and planned to have it for lunch as I was on duty that day. Much to my surprise, when I opened the drawer to get it, the apple was gone! No, it did not make me mad! I simply remarked that I would know who got my apple before the day was over as I had poisoned it. I teased them a lot during the lunch hour. To my surprise, when I arrived at school the next day, there were 15 bright, shiny red apples on my desk. To this day, I do not know who ate my apple. Probably they all took a bite. In fact, I can't remember those who were in this particular class. I just know it happened.

BELIEVE IT OR NOT?

During the '50s when I helped sponsor the 4-H Club, we decided to have a talent show. I contacted students I knew from Rayville and St. Joseph and they helped us spread the word. We had a huge turn-out and netted a fairly large sum of money. The outstanding thing about this event was who appeared on the Epps stage—a group from Ferriday wearing blonde wigs. One played the piano, standing up part of the time and occasionally using his boot on the keyboard. He sang "A Whole Lot of Shaking Going On" and "Great Balls of Fire." Yes, none other than *the* Jerry Lee Lewis! This singer would later give a command performance before the Queen of England and is still very popular today. Ironically, he did not place first. I don't remember who the judges were (just local people), but he was too different and radical for the time. If you don't believe me about this incident, just ask Pat Butts or Buddy Simms. They both tell me they remember. Possibly others do also.

MIRACLES DO HAPPEN!

All "my boys" made the Honor Roll for me during the last six weeks of their high school careers in 1979. They were cronies of Larry's: Cecil Ratliff, Rusty Maples, Curt Ryals and Phillip Parker. I was forever after Larry to study. Somehow, these boys got into the habit of also bringing me their report cards. They even began calling me "Mom." Once I made the error of calling Larry "Puddin Head" in front of them. He almost never lived that down! Larry also made the honor roll two other times: the last six-weeks grading period in 1978, and the last two six-weeks grading periods in 1979.

YES, KIDS (STUDENTS) DO SAY THE DARNDEST THINGS

One day I was lecturing in a bookkeeping class, explaining a new unit, when Lindy Waller raised his hand. I gave him permission to speak. He said, "Miss Clack, what size shoe do you wear?" I told him and kept right on explaining the chapter. I think he has been a principal for sometime at a school in New Orleans.

Another time, many years later, as I was explaining a chapter in bookkeeping, I heard Doodle Johnston whisper, "Look, her legs are not the same size!" And I thought I had their attention. Certainly not his!

MRS. LUSK AND HER ENGLISH CLASS HAD MITES

One day in the old two-story building which no longer exists, I held an English 7th or 8th grade class upstairs. On this particular day, some boy would occasionally slap at his leg, arm, neck or face. I thought they were misbehaving and I corrected them. Some time later, the girls started doing the same thing. I thought I was completely losing control of this class, until the same thing happened to me. Upon close examination, we found "things" crawling on all the desks, and of course, they were getting on us. We called the principal and janitor to come, and they discovered that it was *mites*. It seems bats were roosting in the attic. Of course, word quickly spread throughout the school that Mrs. Lusk and her English class had mites. We all got to go home for the day because we needed to bathe and change clothes. They were literally all over us.

THE GRADE BOOK INCIDENT. THEY WERE CLEVER—BUT THEY GOT CAUGHT!

This is the grade book incident I previously said I would comment on later. This was one incident that "backfired." Earlier I stated that the students were free to look at and average their grades. Once, Barry Cook and Alan Simms changed some of their grades in my grade book. When averaging the grades, I immediately caught the changes. I, of course, had to send them to the office even though I do not recall their punishment. In retrospect, they were clever: very neatly a 75 was made into a 95, a 77 was changed to a 97, a 70 to a 90. I suspect they knew all along that I would catch the changes. Just taking their chances!

LET'S GO TO CROSSETT!
THE ULTIMATUM THAT BACKFIRED

At one point in time, the big thing was to get a group together and drive to Crossett, Arkansas, where on various occasions people declared that they have seen a light on the railroad tracks.

Well, one Friday in typing class, I did not assign any jobs. Some were diligently trying to get their week's work completed, and I told the others to simply practice, type someone a letter, or just keep busy. I kept hearing a whispered word, "Crossett." I called the boys down and told them to get busy. Soon after, I heard another whispered "Crossett." (They were planning a trip for that night.) Once more, I corrected them. Well, it happened again! So, I issued an ultimatum: "O.K., boys," I said. "The very next person I hear say 'Crossett,' I'm going to send out of class."

Well, Barry Cook, who had been busy typing the whole period, looked up and with a questioning look, said "Crossett?" Of course, he had crossed the line. I had issued an *ultimatum*, and I had to send him out of class. To this day, whenever I see him, he greets me with "Let's go to Crossett!" I've received several Christmas cards from him with the same message. Barry has come by to visit several times when he was home.

BASKETBALL STARS

I had many students in typing class who played basketball, and some of them could not resist wadding up their paper and shooting a goal at the wastepaper can. Instead of fighting about it all the time, when they missed they simply had to get up and put the paper in the can. I noticed it was not nearly as much fun when I let them do it.

ON EVALUATIONS

Once when our school was evaluated by a visiting committee, my own sister, Mrs. Caressa Walker of Ouachita Parish High School in Monroe, evaluated my department. I was teased a little about this, but I had nothing to do with it. I also was asked to serve on an evaluation committee for Crowville High School when Dwain Tharpe (a former student) was principal there. I deemed it quite an honor!

HORTICULTURE HINTS

As I have stated, I tried to create a "business atmosphere" in my room. On permanent display were four large letters framed by the Ag department for me. They represented the four styles of business letters, including the three styles of punctuation. They were approximately 3' x 5', and added to the "business" atmosphere I tried to create in my room. Of course, the keyboard was also displayed prominently.

I also had several live plants that seemed to thrive. One year, a group of about five boys asked and got permission to go to my room to type. Mr. Segars approved as long as they were well-behaved. I was in the office that period. I never was aware of any mischief that they got into, because they never bothered any of my things.

In retrospect, I recall how they became quite interested in one of my live plants, a 3' tall dieffenbachia, also called Dumb Cane. "Mrs. Lusk, have you noticed your plant? Maybe it needs some fertilizer or may we water it?" They kept it watered for me, and on several occasions remarked that they thought it really looked sick. Before the school year was over, it actually wilted and died. It was not until years later, at a class reunion, that I learned the true fate of my plant. These boys had chewed tobacco and spit on the soil around my plant. Don Raley and Paul Mercer were the culprits! I wonder why I was not surprised.

THE BLIND BOYS

Each day during the last period that I would spend in my room, I always had volunteers to close the windows (this was before air-conditioning) and adjust my venetian blinds. I'm truly not a perfectionist, but I did like my pictures straight and my blinds even. Of course, they made fun of me. I've actually heard them say, as they sized up the situation, "No, that blind needs to come down about one-fourth inch or no, no, that one is too high." It kept my room neat the way I liked it.

Also, who can forget having to center the carriage, cover the typewriter, close the typing book and place it to the right of the typewriter. Just a routine I demanded. Yes, my room always looked neat!

THE SENIOR TRIP - 1955

Once my husband Bo and I took a group of seniors to New Orleans on their senior trip. Bo drove a school bus for the trip. Knowing the first place they would want to go was Bourbon Street, we had each student get a parent's signature giving us permission to take them down in the French Quarter. I was later told that they did not have any trouble getting their parents to sign as they did not know what Bourbon Street represented.

On this same trip, we spent too much time in the water at Lake Pontchartrain, and we all received too much sun. I actually had to leave school the next day as I could not tolerate clothes touching my back and shoulders. Bubba Kitchens, who was stationed at a nearby airbase, just happened to come with a few friends to the lake this particular weekend. It made it very enjoyable for a lot of the girls.

I recall "Red" Cawthon asked me if he could have a beer-- and that was a no-no! I quickly thought that he would slip and have one anyway so I gave him permission to have only one. He tells me he does not recall this incident. On the trip, we visited a student, Marie Johnston, who was receiving physical therapy there.

I shall never forget Mary Ford's reaction down on Bourbon

Street. All she could say was, "Oh, my, my, Mrs. Lusk; oh, my, my, Mrs. Lusk."

I recall that John Graham kept us laughing almost all the time on the long drive to New Orleans. He was really a "clown."

BLOOPERS

I know I probably committed more bloopers than I can recall. These three stand out in my memory.

1) Carbon Paper Catastrophe

I was sent some samples of smudge-proof carbon paper. Upon demonstrating them to my class, I inadvertently picked up the wrong carbon and proceeded to smear a big black blotch of carbon on my face and wondered why the class found it so funny. I had to be told, "Mrs. Lusk, look in the mirror."

2) The Fire Drill

In writing this book, it dawned on me that BC, as Barry Cook was called, could have easily stood for a headache powder, which I sometimes needed in dealing with him. I have to confess that I remember with fondness those who were the most mischievous. This class was comprised mostly of boys, and they could drive me to distraction at times. I'll never forget the day I *dared* them to say anything. It was just about five minutes until the class would be over. I recall hearing all the commotion in the halls and saw students walking past my door. My class and I sat in my room being very quiet. Finally, BC asked, "Mrs. Lusk, may we leave now or do we just sit here and burn up with the building?" You see, we were having a fire-drill and we almost missed it. Yes, I was teased!

3) Obedience

For many years, we were really crowded in my department. In typing, we had to put two desks together. Each row had six desks with two aisles. This crowded condition made talking to one another very convenient.

One day my students were diligently typing and I was seated very close to them grading papers. Two boys on the front row kept whispering, so I corrected them. I said, "Now, you boys stop typing and start talking." Of course they did just that. So once again, a bit more sternly, I said, "Now you boys simply stop typing and start talking." This they did. Then someone said, "Mrs. Lusk, do you know what you told them to do?" I said, "Yes, I said to stop typing..." and then it dawned on me what I had been saying. Yes, many times the joke has been on me.

THE DUCK CALL

Each year in English class, at some point in time I always introduced a unit on public speaking. They could use objects, drawings, etc., to enhance their reports or speeches. It was strictly oral, they did not have to hand in a written report. I encouraged them to volunteer, get their speech over, and then they could simply relax and enjoy the rest.

This particular unit was well under way one day when the high school supervisor was visiting. My son Daryl was talking about a love of his, duck hunting. He demonstrated the various duck calls on his duck caller.

Of course, the supervisor, Mr. J.L. McKinzie, came to my room to see what was going on as he heard the duck calls while walking down the long hall leading to my room. He told me that actually he had no plans for visiting me that day, but he was so glad that he did. That same day another student, Donna Gwin, gave out her favorite cake recipe and told how to mix and beat the batter, etc. She had also baked the cake and brought it to school, and we all shared a slice of her delicious cake. Don't tell me students can't be innovative! Needless to say, I received a good observation report that day.

THE SWEAT HOGS

In 1979, the year that I retired, I was presented with a problem. A few students needed English III in order to graduate. Would I consent to teaching that class? I had previously taught English 7, 8, and 9--but never English III. I debated and talked Mr. Gwin into giving me all boys, 13 in number. I was not to receive any new students who might transfer or move to Epps. I kept the original 13. I ordered workbooks that were really helpful, and the boys really never gave me much trouble. I had them learn new words, memorize poems, do reports and keep a workbook for a grade--things not necessarily the most fun for them. That's why I was greeted many days with, "How are you, Mrs. Lusk, feeling a little archaic today?" That new word stuck with most of them.

I remember the day I caught Dwain Duckworth cheating as he recited his poem. He got mad and left the class, but returned later, apologized and never gave me any more trouble.

This was when the TV show "Welcome Back Kotter" starring John Travolta was very popular. We were dubbed "The Sweathogs." Actually, they were proud to be called the Sweathogs. I wish to honor them by listing their names. They cooperated with me, even though adjectives and adverbs--in fact, all parts of speech--were not necessarily on their priority list.

My Sweathogs were: Percy Bell, Dwain Duckworth, Doug Ed Fairchild, Andra Gordon, Larry Lusk, Robert McLain, Michael Parker, Grady Porter, Cecil Ratliff, Billy Simms, Donald Sledge, Robert Steimetz and Mike Waller.

For many years, my business department sponsored a contest before the Christmas holidays for the most beautifully decorated door. We had grade school teachers judge all the doors. Would you believe my "Sweathogs" won a ribbon for the "Most Original Door" that year! That really put a feather in their cap. And you know, I more or less enjoyed this unusual class. Certainly a first for me.

NICKNAMES I REMEMBER

I gave three boys a nickname, and to my knowledge, I was the only one to ever call them by these names. Scott Gwin became "Freckles." I said he had stored up meanness for every freckle. I never taught "Freckles," but he was sent to the office all the time. Bennie Wayne Roberson (the second Bennie Roberson) I called "Lasso" because he quite often wore a T-shirt with this logo on it. Mike Prine never failed to say, "Mrs. Lusk, what if I don't finish my job on time? or "What if I don't understand this and can't do it?" So, of course, I called him "What If,' and do so to this day.

Other nicknames (some of them teachers' nicknames) that I remember are listed here. See how many you can identify.

Bodine, Buck, Snake, Bubba, Larry Bud, Satellite, Speedy, Sucky, Martha Washington, Duck, Sugar, Sote, Turk, Punkin, Red, Sag, Sita, Sap, Stinky, Sweet Pea, Deek, Spot, Madam, Juke, Chinaman, Doodle, Rooter, Bud, Merk, Goofus, BC, Kat, Pete, Suzie, Cine, Pud, Sis, Butch, Las Vegas, Hop Sing, Clarabelle, Tiny, Roscoe, Buddy, Cookie, Sucky Earl, Worm, Dobbin, Cotton, Muscles, Bonehead, Old Faithful, TIP, RIP, Chrome Dome, Slick, Tall Mrs. Hawkins, Short Mrs. Hawkins, Ole lady _____, Gay-ree, Catfish, The Preacher, Hawkeye, Hammer, Tiddler, C.C. Rider, Snuffy, Drew, Whitey, Tally, Dino, Wee-Wee, Mick, Wallergater, Birdlegs, Bonnie, Bunting and CY (out of respect for you, I'll not mention your nickname).

MY PHOBIA

I have a phobia about snakes, dating back to when I was a little girl. To this day, I don't look when they are on TV, I've never visited that part of a zoo, and even though it may be only a picture of a snake, I can't bring myself to look at it. You can imagine what happened the day I found a rubber snake in my desk drawer. Obviously, the class could tell I was terrified and that never happened to me again. Thank goodness!

I recall that once Lewis Martin and my sons brought a green snake into my kitchen. My two sons knew, but being boys they wanted to see my reaction. That never happened again!

BRAGGING

Even though Epps is a small school and community, I believe our graduates have gone from here with enough of the basics in education to really make something of themselves. I wish I knew all, but I do know we have doctors, dentists, technicians, teachers in grade school, high school and on the college level, ministers, principals, superintendents, real estate tycoons, insurance agents, bankers, successful farmers, pilots, pharmacists, veterinarians, actors, musicians, dancers, mayors, journalists, newspaper-related jobs, bookkeepers, CPAs, self-employment of various kinds, engineers, nurses, beauticians, aerospace scientists, social workers, policemen, and I'm sure the list could go on and on.

A MOTHER BRAGS

Because I plan on giving my grandchildren an autographed copy of this book, I take the liberty of including this information about my two sons.

DARYL (1977 Graduate)

A "Golden E" award was presented at graduation for athletics.

National Beta Club Honor Society for 4 years.

FFA (3 Years) President and Greenhand

Annual Staff

Voted FHA Beau
Voted Most Talented (Piano)
Voted Best Dressed
Voted Junior Class Favorite

Featured in the 1977 edition of "America's Names and Faces" for outstanding athletic contribution. Baseball: High School and Summer. Pitcher, 3rd Baseman, 1st Baseman, All District (2), District 2-B Champs, 2nd in State, played on all-star teams, attended Baseball Clinic in Baton Rouge
Won numerous local and state 4-H Awards and honors.

LARRY (1979 Graduate)

A "Golden E" award was presented at graduation for outstanding accomplishments in Vocational Agriculture and FFA

FFA Club (4 years), Sentinel (1),
Star Chapter Farmer (3),
Vice-President (2-3),
President (4), Star
Greenhand (1),
Delegate to Leadership
Conference (2),
State Farmer Degree (4),
Plaque for Outstanding
Chapter member (4)

FBLA Club (3-4)
Parliamentarian (4)

Voted Wittiest (2, 3, 4)

Attended Jim Shoulders Bull Riding School in Oklahoma (1977)
Joined Louisiana High School Rodeo Association (2)
Baseball: High School and Summer -
All-Star, First Baseman,
District 2-B Champs, 2nd in State

Won numerous local and state 4-H Awards and honors.

OTHER GOOD GRADES

Because I included students making ½ credit in typing when I taught in Rayville and in St. Joseph, I plan on including Epps students also. Remember, I had a story to tell based on this. I do not mean to embarrass you, just to be fair.

In 1951, Vernon Calcote and Lindy Waller received only ½ credit because they failed to get the required 40 words per minute.

In 1953, those receiving ½ credit were J.T. Kitchens, Vernon Nolan, Julius Raley, Gerald Beasley, Vivian Corley and Jessie Lee Hillman.

In 1954, Charles E. Pruitt received only ½ credit in typing.

In 1955, the trend changed and our guidelines changed. Accuracy was emphasized more and speed did not count as half of the grade, but was averaged in with other grades. I much preferred this method. With the pressure gone, I actually found that I had students excelling in speed.

After remembering all these many incidents about you, I think it only fair to include those of you who made good grades for me! May I take this means to congratulate you! I remember you also, even though you may not have given me "one gray hair." Of course, I'm proud of my B and C students, but plan to list only those of you who made an A for me. I had to draw the line somewhere. The names listed below made an A for their semester grade. If an asterisk (*) appears after a name, that individual had an A for both semesters.

1950 - Semester A's:

Bookkeeping: Elda Glynn Lewis,* Sita Young,* and Morris Ray Plunkett*

Typing I: Roberta Crow,* Jimmie Sue Hammontree,* Fay Auttonberry, Dwain Tharpe,* Bernice Varner and Jo Worthy*

English 8: Bobbie Jean Brock,* Marie Johnston,

65

Mary Ruth Donohue, Shirley Boyette,* Helen Butts, and Noah Lee Hammontree*

1951 - Semester A's:

Bookkeeping: James Burk,* Sharlene Beasley and Ada Lee White

English 8: Marie Brock, Avie Nell Kennedy and Gloria Tatum*

Typing I: Sharline Beasley,* Sarah Tatum,* Sybil Ann Gilmore,* Marcelain Kitchens, Elda Glynn Lewis,* Sita Young,* Barbara Hale, J.L. Smith and Minnie Lou McPherson

1952 - Semester A's:

Bookkeeping: Evelyn Beasley, Laverne Newton, Maurice Nelson and J.L. Smith*

Typing I: Ada Lee White,* Evelyn Beasley, Wanda Rose Prine* and Betty Jo Raley*

English 8: Jean Adams,* Jimmy Holmes* and Joyce Smith*

1953 - Semester A's:

Typing I: Bobbie Jean Brock,* Shirley Boyette,* Jean Richmond and Hazel Pickering

Bookkeeping: Shirley Boyette* and Irene Hearne

English 8: Sammie Lane Dickens,* June Dale Hillman, Jackie Tharpe* and Ruth Thornton

1954 - Semester A's:

English 8: Andy Barham,* Linda Hale* and June Pruitt

Shorthand: Shirley Boyette,* Sara Jo Calhoun, Hazel Pickering* and Jean Richmond

Typing I: Maxine Traxler

Bookkeeping: Bobbie Jean Brock,* Maxine Traxler,* Gay Whitaker* and Helen Butts

1955 - Semester A's:

Typing I: Jimmy Holmes, Leathie Crawley,* Jean Adams, Patricia Ezell and Toni Newton*

General Business: Toni Newton,* Maxine Sherman and Maxine Traxler

Shorthand: Maxine Sherman* and Maxine Traxler

Bookkeeping: None

1956 - Semester A's:

Typing I: Alice Sherman,* Jackie Tharpe,* John Mercer, Robin Newton,* Jean Sealy* and Ruth Thornton

General Business: Voncille Ezell

Bookkeeping: Jean Adams, Toni Newton,* Alice Ruth Butts, and Leathie White

1957   -   Semester A's:

Typing I: Pat Butts* and Glenda Thrower*

Shorthand: Robin Newton,* Alice Sherman,* Jackie
Tharpe* and Ruth Thornton*

Bookkeeping: Annie Ruth Gwin,* Robin Newton,*
Jean Sealy,* Alice Sherman,* Jackie Tharpe* and
Ruth Thornton*

English 7: Sharon Snider*

1958   -   Semester A's:

Typing I: Margaret Ann Reeves* and Mildred
Hendrix

Shorthand: Glenda Thrower,* Linda Hale and Patsy
Tanner

Bookkeeping: Pat Butts, Linda Hale* and Glenda
Thrower*

1959   -   Maternity Leave

1960   -   Semester A's:

Bookkeeping: Mary Allen Sealy* and Jarvis
Thomas*

Typing I: Mary Ann Guice, Larry Hopper, Delores
Sistrunk and Gerrie Simms

English 7: Mary Margaret Davis,* Joe Gilmore* and
Wayne Tanner*

Spelling: Melba Black,* Carol Corbin,* Mary Margaret Davis,* Joe Gilmore,* Jeanette Hale* and Wayne Tanner*

1961 - Maternity Leave

1962 - Semester A's:

Typing I: Lexie Derrick,* June Fryer,* Charles Rider,* Eileen Butler,* Francine Corley,* Sonny Felker,* Donna Hogan,* Ronnie Jackson,* Paul Mercer, Judy Simms* and Mike Newton

Shorthand: June Fryer, Kay Griffin* and Cherry Hawkins*

Bookkeeping: Kay Griffin* and Cherry Hawkins*

1963 - Semester A's:

Typing I: Charleace Hinton,* Gary Miller,* Charlie Smith, Jami Jones* and Reba Trapp

English 7: None

Shorthand: Eileen Butler, Leatrice Calhoun, Francine Corley,* Pam Donohue* and Judy Simms*

Bookkeeping: Donna Hogan,* Ronnie Jackson* and Judy Simms*

1964 - Semester A's:

Bookkeeping: Charleace Hinton,* Jami Jones,* Gary Miller* and Kathaleen Walters

Typing I: Melba Black, Mary Margaret Davis,*
Jeanette Hale,* Carolyn Weatherly,* Nina Powell
and Jo Ann Simms*

Shorthand: Sue Bunker,* Charleace Hinton,* Jami
Jones,* Judy Stewart and Kathaleen Walters

1965   -   Semester A's:

Typing I: Karlene Cook,* Joycelyn McDermitt,*
Max Reeves and Paul Gowan*

English 9:   None

Shorthand: Mary Margaret Davis,* Jeanette Hale,*
Elaine Wagnon and Carolyn Tarver*

Bookkeeping: Jeanette Hale, Wayne Tanner* and
Elaine Wagnon*

1966   -   Semester A's:

Typing I: Rhonda Chelette,* William Copeland,
Pam Oliphant,* Bonnie Holley, Janice Owens,* Jo
Ann Plunkett and Glenda Prine*

Bookkeeping: Karlene   Cook*   and   Joycelyn
McDermitt*

Shorthand: Virginia Guice, Barbara Johnson,*
Danny   Jones,   James   Kitchens,*   Joycelyn
McDermitt* and Ruth Wingfield*

1967   -   Semester A's:

Typing I: Gary Crouch,* Phil Jackson* and Arlene
McPherson

Shorthand: Rhonda Chelette,* Bonnie Holley* and Pam Oliphant*

Bookkeeping: Pam Oliphant,* David Jones and Glenda Prine*

1968 - Semester A's:

Shorthand: Lucy Navarro* and Doris Landers

Typing I: Sue Black,* Connie Carter, David Duckworth, Allen Latch, Karen Prine and Donna Ratliff*

Bookkeeping: Gary Crouch* and Arlene McPherson

1969 - Semester A's:

Clerical Practice: Sue Black,* Connie Carter and Vickie Prine

Bookkeeping: Karen Prine

Typing I: Pam Hale

1970 - Semester A's:

Clerical Practice: Shirley Coleman and Pam Hale

Bookkeeping: Tommy Powell and Sue Black

Typing I: None

1971 - Semester A's:

Clerical Practice: Sonja Segars and Connie Lewis

Shorthand: Donna Duckworth, Kathy Farish,* Marilyn Johnson and Connie Lewis

Bookkeeping: Donna Duckworth,* Marilyn Johnson and Kathy Farish*

1972 - Semester A's:

Bookkeeping: Mike McPherson

Shorthand: Ann Skipper and Debbie Davis

1973 - Semester A's:

Shorthand: Gail Moseley,* Joy Black and Penny Prine

English 8: Donna Gwin,* Fay Hall,* Kay Hall,* Dawn Waller,* Kim Kitchens, Gail Lingefelt and Daryl Lusk

Spelling: Johnny Bams,* Donna Gwin,* Fay Hall,* Kay Hall,* Brenda Henderson,* Andy Johnston,* Kim Kitchens,* Daryl Lusk,* Bobby Runions,* Dawn Waller,* Herman Bell, Mickey Black, Cindy Corley, Deborah Hall, Anna Jean McPherson, Gail Lingefelt, Cynthia Roberts, Roy Smith and Bobby Sam Gwin.

Bookkeeping: Jeanette Hines* and Leslie McDermitt*

1974 - Semester A's:

Bookkeeping: Sharron Carter, Glenda Guice,* Kathy Cleveland,* Janice Prine* and Stephanie Waller

English 8: Terri Hillman,* Donna Roberson,* Janet White* and Annette Runions

Spelling: Ricky Barnes,* Darrye Clark,* Carl Gwin,* Terri Hillman,* Jody Johnston,* Sarah Mobley,* Donna Roberson,* Cynthia Roberts,* Annette Runions,* Janet White,* Carol Philley, Robin Black, Erma Brown and Rise Miller

Clerical Practice: Nona Cawthon,* Kathy Ratliff, Stephanie Waller,* Kay Wilson and Chris King

1975 - Semester A's:

Typing I: Denise Boyette,* Becky Swett* and Sharon Waller*

Clerical Practice: None

Journalism: Dorothy Collins,* Debbie Monroe,* Kathy Ratliff,* Lovely Bams, Brenda Barnes, Lynn Fryer, Sarah Henderson, Charles Johnston, Kathy Nielson, Janice Prine, Becky Swett and Stephanie Waller

Bookkeeping: Dorothy Collins, Walter Jones,* Lewis Martin, Kathy Ratliff* and Tommy Smith

1976 - Semester A's:

Typing I: Erma Brown,* Darrye Clark,* Connie Gwin,* Anis Martin,* Julie Nielsen,* Bobby Runions,* Pam Waller, Elizabeth Weatherly,* Lisa Cawthon,* Cindy Corley,* Donna Gwin,* Fay Hall,* Kay Hall,* Terri Hillman,* Andy Johnston, Julie Jones,* Kim Kitchens,* Pat Lingefelt,* Daryl Lusk,* Lewis Martin, Annette Runions,* Dawn

Waller,* Robin Black, Wayne McMillan, Loretta May, Mike Prine and Johnny Bams.

Bookkeeping: Sherry Hillman,* Kathy Nielsen* and Sue Ratliff*

Journalism: Debra Barnes,* Denise Boyette,* Billy Day,* Jeff Fox,* and Sue Ratliff*

Clerical Practice: Kathy Nielsen* and Becky Swett*

1977 - Sabbatical Leave

1978 - Semester A's:

Typing I: Todd Bastion,* Robin Fryer,* Richard Hillman,* Lucius Hopkins, Robert Jones,* Clem Marshall, Lisa Scriber,* Lisa Smith,* Russell Williams, Cindy Beard, Doug Ed Fairchild, Jeff Guice, Carolyn Holman, Bessie Humes,* Joe Ann Humes, Delores McGhee, Leonard Rhymes,* Robert Steinmetz* and Cynthia Thompson

Bookkeeping: Connie Gwin,* Marilyn Jones, Anis Martin,* Donna Roberson,* Pam Waller, Elizabeth Weatherly* and Janet White*

Shorthand: Erma Brown,* Darrye Clark,* Rise Miller, Terri Hillman,* Jody Johnston, Loretta May* and Donna Roberson

Clerical Practice: Erma Brown,* Darrye Clark,* Jody Johnston, Cheryl McPherson,* Loretta May,* Julie Nielsen,* Donna Mobley, Lisa Simms* and Pam Waller*

1979 - Semester A's:

Clerical Practice: Todd Bastion,* Richard Hillman,* Leonard Rhymes,* Anis Martin* and Russell Williams

Bookkeeping: Jimmy Jones,* Robert Jones,* Cheryl McPherson,* Fannie Gray, Clem Marshall, Julie Nielsen,* Leonard Rhymes* and Lisa Scriber

Typing I: Sonja Fox,* Lisa Hale, Walter Hillman, Bruce Johnson, Linda McCann, Mary Martin,* Laney Rhymes,* Mary Beth Beard,* Debra Collier,* Marsha Harris,* Glen McCandlish, Jan Corley, Vickie Mobley and Dana Simms

English III: Robert Steimetz

CONFESSIONS...by CHRIS
(My Memoirs)

Because there is no risque event or incident to include, I've tried to add a few intriguing incidents and thoughts for your enjoyment. Actually, I'm striving to capture your attention! May you enjoy and smile.

Somehow three students, who will remain nameless, seemed to be favorites of mine. After attending several reunions, it finally dawned on me as to the reason. They crossed my path before the love of my life entered. If we had met under different circumstances, I probably could have become "interested" in them. I'm not really sure they will know I'm speaking about them, but I have a feeling they might. (Remember, I taught at Rayville, St. Joe and Epps before I married in 1952.)

Yes, I did date a student I had taught, but it was after he graduated and was attending college. By the way, he was the only former student I ever dated. We have remained good friends through the years. And yes, for intrigue he will remain nameless. (Continued in Afterthoughts)

When I was young and unattached, a few teachers met with

the students at Malissa's (the local hangout) after the ballgames and replayed the games. Remember Fay Miller, Coach Dolores Carter and me?

Also, in 1950 or 1951, I was actually asked to be in the Miss Louisiana Pageant. I was dating a boy from Winnsboro and he told the Winnsboro Jaycees about me. Was I surprised when someone came to school to ask me to enter. Flattering, of course, but no way! I had no talent and was not such a beauty either. They must have been really desperate that year. This was when the pageants were held outdoors in Lake Providence. The setting was beautiful and I always attended.

Believe it or not, six weeks after I started dating Bo, we were planning our wedding. I wanted to wait until June when school would be out, but he won this argument. In all the rush, he did not know my ring size. We were to be married on Saturday, March 8, 1952. On Friday, he came to the school to get my ring size. Mr. Gilmore, my principal, used that big set of ring sizers and measured my finger for my wedding ring. Naturally, I did not help pick it out. I always jokingly said, "I know it was a real diamond, for it was too small to have a flaw in it." I treasured it then, and it is among my keepsakes even now.

COMMENTS ON C. W. GILMORE

Mrs. Holmes, the English teacher and librarian, sent Sybil Ann Gilmore to the office one day to report a missing book. She rushed in and told her dad that *The Yearling* was lost. He looked over toward his house and remarked, "Oh, my goodness, I guess Ole Sam left the gap down." He thought she was talking about his calf.

Being the efficient secretary that I tried to be, one day I proceeded to clean and rearrange his desk in an orderly fashion. He called me into his office and very kindly said, "Mrs. Lusk, you really did a nice job and it looks great, I just can't find anything. Next time, please leave my desk alone when you want to rearrange it." It simply amazed me, but he could retrieve any item he wanted with his method, which was to have piles and piles of letters, papers and books all in disarray on his desk. Needless to say, I never bothered his desk again!

He was, in my opinion, a man before his time. His mind worked like a computer before computers were in common use. He could recall an incident or date without thinking, recite poetry, and as he aged I do believe his mind became even keener. I recall with fondness the monologue he did so well in costume. He performed it for me at one of our banquets.

When I first started helping in the office (upstairs in the two-story building). I would work on one side of Mr. Gilmore's desk. By the way, this is the desk that I now own. It was last period one day and a very attractive lady had been visiting, promoting some show that the school agreed to sponsor. Many shows were booked back then, some educational and some just fun. The lady had just left the office and was taking the two flights of stairs down to the first floor. The last bell rang for school to be dismissed before she had time to get to the first floor. My, the noise that the hurried feet made on those old wooden steps! I'll never forget this day as he looked at me with a twinkle in his eye and commented, "I surely hope she makes it."

COMMENTS ON J. D. SEGARS

At teachers' meetings when he issued a rule, he was always right. He would never admit to being wrong. But on occasions I would say, "I think if enough would sign a petition, he might change his mind." They did and he would! That way he was able to "save face." This is the first time I've admitted to doing this for he asked me not to tell.

We kept everything filed. We updated the system and gave every student an individual folder. He kept all dates and happenings filed. For example, he could tell you when the Garden Club landscaped the school campus, when the magnolia tree was planted and much more trivia.

I think more for his own enjoyment, as well as because it was pertinent information, he kept a file on all teachers. He loved to put the most unflattering school picture of us he could find into this folder. Just ask Lou Miller, if you doubt this. He used to laugh and comment, "These are my blackmail files." I wonder if those files still exist.

If you went by his handwriting, Mr. Segars should have been a doctor. I don't know if he was good at spelling or not. He often left letters and notes for me to type for him. Many words were started and then the squiggling would begin. I soon learned to decipher these words and somehow typed a mailable letter. Luckily, I never had to retype one.

There were times, however, when our individual systems of filing clashed. I remember the day the health nurse came to recheck some students with a hearing loss. I looked under the headings Hearing, Speech and Health Nurse, and finally called him in the gym with my problem. He said, "Stupid, look under Ear." Obvious, of course! Stupid was one of his favorite words and you just learned not to take it personally. Really, he truly did not mean it in a derogatory way.

When I first came to Epps, he asked me for dates many times, but he was simply not my type. We did, however, become really good friends.

Once when he was dating a lady from Jackson, Mississippi, he asked me to get a large box of chocolate candy and wrap it really pretty for him. Well, my office helper and I did just that-- and much to my surprise, he had had me wrap my own gift. Needless to say, I was surprised! He was very unpredictable.

Quite often he would leave on my desk some correspondence he wanted me to do for him. Often times, he would not be in the office when I actually did the work. Once he left a book with instructions to order the items checked. I ordered an electric pencil sharpener and a paper shredding machine. It rather puzzled me that he was spending money on such items. I knew I had "been had" when the next item was for a portable john! Many of you will not realize that he possessed this sense of humor. He was a delight to work for in the office. He also liked music and we often had background music as we carried on our work.

As I have stated previously, among other jobs I kept two sets of books. One set was for the general fund and one was for the athletic department. We did business with several sporting and athletic companies in Monroe. One of them, and I won't state which one, simply could not keep our books and checks straight with their invoices. Every so often, Mr. Segars would give me the day off and I would take my invoices and books to their company to help them reconcile our accounts. (We were always correct.) Quite often, he would give me gas and lunch money for the trip to Monroe. I usually stopped by for my mother, and after completing my business, we could shop till we dropped!

Sometimes, as many of us do, he found it hard to remember a name. A Mrs. Latch moved into our community and he often saw her when the buses were loading for the end of the school day. He associated the word *gate* with *latch* to help him remember her name. Yes, you guessed it, he greeted her by saying, "Hello, Mrs. Gate, how are you?"

COMMENTS ON DON GWIN

My work load was not as busy in the office as it had once been. During Don's tenure, teachers' aides were hired. The year I took a sabbatical, Mable Jackson was hired as the first full-time school secretary. After this, for two years I did not work in the office.

During this time, the school board mandated that principals must, among their other duties, observe the teachers in their classrooms. I could tell that this was one of Don's duties that he did not particularly like. He gave me my favorite report, writing Satisfactory on all categories and noting "Very" next to the column on appearance, personality and attitude.

Don discovered that he had the kind of sweet corn that I dearly love. It reminds me of the corn my dad always planted. For several years now, he has shared bountifully with me and will take no pay. So I take him several loaves of my homemade bread that I give to special friends. His granddaughter Samantha loves it. Now I make sure I bake a loaf or two for her when she's visiting. She calls me "the bread lady."

One year I drove Don to school as it was difficult for him to ride a school bus with a broken leg. At that time, neither of us would have imagined in our wildest dreams that he would later become my principal.

COMMENTS ON INTEGRATION

In 1970, our school was integrated for the first time, in grades 9-12. I for one did not know what to expect. I had not been around many blacks in my former years. I had a black co-worker, Miss Irma Christian, and I could not have asked for a more cooperative and likable person with which to share my department. She and I got along fabulously.

As for the students, I found them to be just your average teenagers. I believe many of them learned to like me as much as did my students in previous years. They respected me, and like the ones who had preceded them, some were good students and some were "goof-offs." It was interesting to learn of the differences in our cultures. They learned from us and we certainly learned from them.

At first, many of them just naturally missed their former school, as they had had to move into our school. They were used to more parties and, of course, no two schools have the same extra-curricular activities.

Mr. Segars was principal in 1970 when the school was first integrated in grades 9-12. He retired in 1971 and Mr. Donald R. Gwin became principal in 1972. I give him much credit for our school never having any serious racial problems. In fact, I'm proud of both our white and black students who learned to co-exist in harmony.

NO EDUCATION

I taught five years without any education or student teaching. Actually I had fun making this statement. Let me explain. To qualify to teach, one had to have not only subjects in a chosen field, but several semester hours or courses called Education. Most were just "fluff" in my opinion. The two courses I took which actually helped me were called "Tests and Measurements" and "Adolescent Psychology." You were required to get a teacher's certificate. I taught each year and attended summer school at Louisiana State University in Baton Rouge each summer. Student teaching was never offered in the summer, so if you had taught for five years and had a good "track record" you would be observed in your classroom at your school. In 1952, I was observed by Mr. J. E. Williams from the State Department in Baton Rouge and Mr. C. L. Madden from LSU. By this method, I received college credit for Student Teaching and finished all other work in the summer. When I transferred from the College of Business to the College of Education, I lost 30 hours. I had to make these up and also take the required Education courses. I ended up being qualified to teach all Business subjects plus English and Speech.

In my "off" subject (English), I really tried. In college, we each had to have a certain number of semester hours in English. It just was not a favorite course to teach. I think the ages of my students had a lot to do with this. You see, I liked all my students, but preferred the older ones.

After getting in front of a class in high school to give a report and completely "drawing a blank," I promised that in college I would take a few Speech courses. That's how I ended up with a major in Business and a minor in Speech. I suppose that is why I was never ill at ease in front of my classes, but to face a large crowd was not, and to this day still isn't, my forte.

THE MISFIT

I've always been a "misfit," but you know I did not mind. Many of my dresses were made by a local seamstress. (I have been known to pay more for the patterns than for the fabric.) I did not like to meet myself coming around the corner, so to speak. Clothes that were a little different and stylish were my preference.

Once my boys were invited to a birthday party, and it was soon discovered that I had taught all the mothers in attendance. You see, I started my family when I was 32 years old.

I stayed in a Young Married Sunday School Class until I retired. Then it dawned on me that it would not be "politically correct" to be retired and still in a "young" class so I moved on up to the next level. I adjust easily, and no one had ever seemed to mind that I was the "old" one. In fact, in my immediate family, at this time in our lives, my husband and I are the "old folks." Neither of us really think of ourselves in this way. Do you suppose I'll ever grow up?

This remark was meant for me and I know who said it, but I'll not tell: "You know, that's a long time to be a good girl." I was twenty-five years old when I married. Also, another time and another remark: "If I thought I had a chance that she'd go with me, I'd be knocking on her door tonight."

They might remember saying these things, and then again, they may not. I really never knew for sure if they knew I heard these remarks. Remember, you learn to ignore some incidents. (The last remark has been verified, but to keep things intriguing, he will remain nameless.)

One other incident was overheard in the hall: a Hale boy remarking about Erline Jones, who did have a wiggle in her walk, "If my old mule had that kind of walk, I'd plow the sucker to death!"

When I bump into former students and they call me Miss Clack, that really dates me.

Once, I sent food to a home where there was a death in the family and Maxine Boyette said she recognized my handwriting.

Since graduating in 1951, Elda Glyn Lewis has not missed a year in sending me a birthday card. I eagerly anticipate getting it every year!

Sonny Felker and Dorothy Adams tell me they named their children after me: Christina and Layne (my middle name). I have met Tina Felker and deem it a real honor to have two namesakes. My only other namesake is one of my granddaughters whose middle name is Christine.

I used to wear only one perfume, Tabu, and have been told by several that this fragrance always reminds them of me. Poor students, I loved it and wore it all year, and as many of you will know, it has a rather strong fragrance. I suppose I had a lipstick shade, shoes and pencils to exactly match most of my outfits. I had this habit of having a pencil behind my ear--it always matched or did not clash with the color I had chosen for the day. I also loved large purses (still do). I recall one skit about teachers in which they called my purse a feedbag. Someone also remarked that I had lost a typewriter somewhere in the vicinity of my handbag.

I loved earrings and still do today. I fondly remember when I wear a pair that was given to me by my students.

Now that I'm retired, I find that I love all fragrances and basically use only two shades of lipstick. Especially when traveling, I have one lipstick for reds and one lipstick for the pinks and purples. Time does change things!

You know, for many, many years we lived in a house with only one bathroom; somehow, my two sons and I got dressed and made it to school on time. I was never late for school. It boggles my mind now how I pulled off this feat!

For one or two years, it was popular for students to give their teachers an Appreciation Card when they graduated. I have cards from Mike Jones, Joe Gilmore, Wayne Tanner, David Jones, Janie Carter, Pat Lingefelt, Mary Margaret Davis, Leonard Rhymes, Laney Rhymes, Ronnie Jackson, Marilyn Thompson, Kathy Lingefelt, Janice Lingefelt and Sherry Lynn Neal. I am very appreciative of having received these cards and I sincerely hope that I did not misplace one.

Some students gave me pictures of their children, visited me with their children or just simply stopped by to see me. They included:

> Chris and Bill Duckworth's son
> Dana and Carl Gwin's children, Kevin and Kristy
> Mikey Coleman's daughter
> Kelly Swett
> Angela Boykin
> Shaun Steven Smith
> Kaya McKnight
> Melanie Martin
> Veronica Lyn Rochelle
> Angela Lingefelt
> Katee Fairchild

Stacie Lingefelt
Ben Stage and Julie
Candy Jones and boys
Channing Dorr

Bo and I used to babysit Melanie Martin before we had grandchildren of our own. We fondly refer to her as our "first granddaughter." She was the daughter of Lewis and Karen Edwards Martin. Several other students visited me often and I'm sorry to say that some of them are no longer married, including:

Craig and Linda Matthews Hale
Bruce and Debbie Sewell
Denise Boyette and Danny Whitaker
Randy and Annette Sullivan McCalmon
Malcolm and Judy Matthews Butler
Lewis and Karen Martin.

Others to visit at various times were:
Barry Cook
The Hall family
The Black family
Ray Hemphill
Linda Coody (she calls frequently from Kansas)
Bill Smith (he calls occasionally from South Carolina)
Brenda Jean McCalmon
Brenda Sue Hale
Sandra Hale
Glenda Thrower
Karen Boykin
Doris Landers
Sonny Felker
Elsie Lee Coody
Betty Lou "Pete" Nelson (by phone)
Alice Andrews
Craig Yates
Curt Ryals
Mickey Black

Ronnie Kitchens
J. T. Kitchens
Lewis Martin
Terry McKnight
Tommy Tanner

Many students live in and around Epps, and I get to see them and their children often.

Linda Coody, a former student who helped me and kept my boys, now calls me her "Other Mother." Both of her parents are now dead, and I've become a substitute for someone from home. She lives in Kansas and calls me rather often or writes. She also visits when she is home. My boys dearly loved her. She would bake cookies or do anything else they wanted.

I usually tried to use student help and have been pleased with all who worked for me and kept my sons: Becky and Debbie Monroe, Wanda Hall, Rhonda Brock, Janice and Kathy Lingefelt, Bonnie Weatherly (I hope I remembered all)...and then there was Karen Boykin.

Karen Boykin helped me all one summer after I had surgery. She was great! Her boyfriend was Terry McKnight who was a big buddy of my boys. He was older, but he kept his horse "Midnight" in a pasture behind our house and visited us quite often. They finally married, but I recall one time when they broke-up and stopped by to tell me all about their love life. They have been happily married for many years now, have two children and a beautiful home. You can see why I claim both of them.

After retirement, one of the very best to ever help me clean house was Darrye Clark. She helped me for several years. I had previously been helped by her grandmother, Velvet, and grew to love her very much.

One summer I was at school for one of my Extended Summer School classes and got to pick the colors to repaint my classroom. I chose a dusty rose and a muted blue which complemented each other. Thank goodness I was there. My room could have been painted "swimming pool green." I like green, but not that shade. I most likely would have been nauseated.   Once during one of my pregnancies, I became nauseated in a room at home which had green drapes.

Through the years I have received many varied gifts from individual students, and sometimes the class as a whole would give me a nice gift. One that I remember is an oil painting of a panther in Epps High School colors of black and gold that was given to me by Jeff Fox. It hangs in my game room today. He also painted the Seal of the United States. I have it, Jeff, just never got around to having it framed.

Several pairs of earrings were given to me, and I remember who gave me most of them. Gaye Whitaker, Janie Carter and the Coleman boys gave me earrings and pins, and I think of them whenever I wear them. Sometimes the earrings would be from the entire class and I recall this when I wear them. Sorry, just can't remember which class.

Wall plaques were given to me by Becky Monroe, Sue Ratliff and Jan Corley. I have crochet given to me by Ruthie McPherson and several records were given to me by Dorothy Skipper. Another gift was a pair of Dutch figurines, kissing each other. They were really salt and pepper shakers. One class gave me a baby silver spoon and fork in my chosen pattern. After Daryl's first child arrived, I gave them to him. I'm sorry to say the spoon had had to survive a whirl in the disposal.

I have a Christmas wreath made entirely of plastic, given to me by Nona Gale Cawthon. I decorated it with the plastic ornaments my boys first used to "decorate and redecorate" the Christmas tree. Some evenings when I came home from school, all the ornaments might be in the waste basket. The next day they could be found hanging in disarray on only one side of the tree. It became a very treasured keepsake.

Both Helen Fryer and Sandra Gowan gave me rings. Maxine Gowan, an adult, gave me a silver bracelet. She attended one of my typing classes. The students accepted her as one of them. Julie Neilsen and Glynn Hale gave me figurines of an old woman and man. They were so cute. Janie Carter gave me yellow earrings and a pin to match. She worked in the office with me and kept me well informed. (She knew *everything*!)

The Rhymes boys, Leonard and Laney, gave me a very

unique nail polish bottle holder, which I use often. One class gave me a pair of silver earrings with many colored stones that dangle. They are one of my favorites.

Roland Carter, the ring and invitation salesman for many years. always told Mr. Segars in my presence, "It must be something in the water here, for all the women on your faculty are pretty." I simply accepted it for what it was, a nice compliment. Sexual harassment never entered my mind.

My granddaughter Taffy recently told me that a former student of mine who is now a teacher, Mrs. Carolyn Simms Guchereau, said to her, "We got more speed on the old manual typewriters that we had to use than you all are getting on the computers."

My usual comment when given a compliment was, "I thank you, that's worth an 'A', but I don't have my grade book with me." Debbie Monroe told me, "Mrs. Lusk, you *always* say that."

A few other special students were: Nina Powell, Rise Miller, Pina Pruett, Kim Kitchens, Dawn Waller, Eileen Butler, Gayla Hale, Gwen Miller and Bobbie Jean Brock, among a host of others.

I completely forgot a faculty meeting only one time in my teaching career. It was here in Epps. I even wondered as I passed the school to go "up town" what all the cars were doing there. Not until the next day when I was reminded did I remember. Was my face red!

Because I related so well to the teen-agers in my classes, I really was not the least bit apprehensive about our own sons becoming teen-agers. Was I in for a surprise! I remember when they were young, I told my husband to please not let me make them "sissies." No worry! It was not too long before I was saying, "Please, God, help me to civilize them!"

We speak of the music played in the '50s, '60s and '70s and how we could not relate to some of it or even understand it. But I believe most kids like a little rude humor. Remember that imperishable ditty (sung to the tune of *The Old Gray Mare:* "Great green gobs of greasy, grimy gopher guts, mutilated monkey feet…"? I threatened many times to send my boys and their friends away from the table.

I recall singing as a youngster the silly ditty "Mairzy doats and does eat oats and little lambs eat ivy" as well as "Two little fishes, or was it three, that swam and swam all over the dam." We must remember that we too were young once. In my opinion, that is where many teachers fail. One cannot expect perfection all the time.

Craig Yates spent so much time at our house with our boys that his mother said she should give me his birth certificate.

Curt Ryals and our son Larry were great buddies. I'm truly grateful that I do not know all the mischief in which they were involved. On graduation night, Curt came here to get Bo to help with his tie. I suppose I will always remember Curt, Larry and Daryl's hunting and all the doves and duck gumbo I've cooked for them. Those were really the good old days!

Once Dwain Duckworth stopped by and we were having fresh strawberry pie. He must have really enjoyed it as he said to me, "Mrs. Lusk, if I will buy the strawberries, will you make me a pie?" He did…and I did. Afterwards, he brought me a can of ribbon cane syrup and remarked, "I ate the entire pie and a half gallon of ice cream at one time."

Recently, quite by accident, I met Martha Willis Till who took my place on my first maternity leave. I chat with her often. She says she has fond memories of teaching here at Epps.

I give much credit and thanks to Donna Mobley and Cheryl McPherson, who would take turns making a carbon copy of their American history notes, bringing them to me, and saying, "Mrs. Lusk, make Larry study these notes tonight. We have a test tomorrow." I felt that is why he passed American history. After graduation, I told Larry he owed them a steak dinner. I believe he did take them out to eat.

James Kitchens and I were two of those who still remained "young at heart." Each winter, we both wished for a wonderland of white. In fact, only this year I received an early morning call from him one Sunday. He said, "Sorry to wake you, but look out the window." Then he hung up. It was the most beautiful sight with snow and ice everywhere, and it only lasted through the morning. We never receive much snow in any given year.

In planning for my retirement, I knew I would need to be

with and around people. One year I traced my family tree so I would be eligible to join the local Daughters of the American Revolution (DAR). I became really interested in genealogy. With the help of a friend who is a professional genealogist, I was able to document my family tree back to the 1600s, which also made me eligible for the Colonial Dames of the XVII Century. I discovered that an ancestor of mine had fought with George Washington at Valley Forge, which made me eligible for Descendants of Washington's 'Army at Valley Forge. This more or less boggles my mind as I always used to say, "I don't particularly like history. I'd rather *make* it than study it!" I much preferred the subject of geography.

I was a charter member of the Epps Garden Club and was active for 28 years. I didn't like the horticulture part and my yard was good evidence of that. I did, however, like the artistic design part and won many ribbons for flower arranging. I also won two Tri-Colors, two Sweepstakes Awards, and I am most proud of winning two Creativity Awards.

After retirement, I discovered that I like the crime and courtroom scenes in such shows as Columbo and Matlock. And of course I get to watch lots of westerns, thanks to my cowboy husband. It took me four years before I could get interested in the soaps and watched only one of them on occasion. I love music and kept that on most of the time. I also discovered I liked Louis L' Amour novels and books by Danielle Steele and Rosamunde Pilcher. I also became very interested in Bible prohecy and have read most of Hal Lindsey's works.

My last year of teaching school was most enjoyable, with no office work, no banquets, no report cards, and no register to keep. I only had to teach my classes and sponsor the FBLA club. I had a new department which took in Mrs. Gilmore's math room, extending my department farther to the north into what was once the high school library. This was done in 1978. A bookcase with a countertop was used as a room divider. I now had three doors, ample storage, and I could walk around all the desks. We were not so crowded. My last period class helped me mark off the calendar which showed the countdown to my retirement.

The first person to see me (without make-up) after retirement was James Kitchens. He said he almost didn't recognize me. It was late and I thought I could simply slip into the grocery store without being seen by anyone. I've learned that rarely happens.

My granddaughters kept saying, "Nanny, how can you say you are a former business teacher and not even own a computer?" So I did buy one. Computers had not been introduced into our country schools before I retired. Well, reading *Windows for Dummies* didn't do a thing for me other than make me feel like a dummy. As Nicholas Negroponte, the founder and director of the Massachusetts Institute of Technology (MIT) Media Laboratory, a research center, says, "The advice that I give has always been the same and it sounds a little coy: Get a kid. They're the experts!" I feel lucky that I have two teenagers nearby who have promised to help me get online, or as they like to say, "plug and play." Wish me luck!

I must believe in long distance moves. Many of you may remember that when I first married we stayed in an apartment just off the school campus. Later our first home was built on the adjoining lot west of the apartment. Years later, we built our present home across the street almost directly in front of the first home.

I must tell you this historical data about the lot on which my home is located. First, much fill-in dirt was hauled from an Indian mound that a farmer had leveled near the present Poverty Point site. Before we built, this lot was used by our own boys and the neighborhood boys as a baseball diamond, a football field, a golf course, and a launching pad. A neighbor boy, Danny Whitaker, built a rocket and launched it from this vacant lot. It actually took off into the air for several yards. We deemed it a huge success!

The most infamous incidents were the many black walnut fights my boys had (without my permission). You know something about this, don't you, Little Bill (Kitchens)? The good Lord was surely watching over them, for a rather large black walnut could have really injured an eye.

Bo and I, throughout our married life, have had no real conflicts. The thing I do that "bugs" him the most is my insistence that he look at me when I'm talking to him. He says it's the schoolteacher coming out in me. Of course, I insist that he is really not listening to me if he is watching the TV. Imagine Sheldon E. or Malcolm B. looking out the window when I had called their names and was talking directly to them! I feel that sometimes they were looking directly at me and not hearing a word I was saying anyway. And this statement could go for many others.

I tried to be a Christian witness to my students. Many of them confided in me and I tried to give them good advice. One time a certain girl, one of my favorites, told me that if I did not go to the Beta Convention with them, her folks would not let her go. I considered that a very nice compliment, but this is the first time I've ever told anyone about this incident. I certainly did not want to seem to be bragging.

Once, during a revival at church, we were asked to invite someone to the services. I took advantage of being a teacher and announced in my classes the invitation for them to attend. Was I surprised and was my heart warmed when a host of my students stood up saying I had invited them. I won that contest, and the prize was a book called "Making the Most of the Time." It was a timely book.

We know we live in a world that is aware of time. When I retired, one of the first things I did was to take off my watch. I no longer had to be at a certain place at a certain time. Several years went by before I started wearing a watch again. Just one of my silly "idiosyncrasies."

I do not know how it is now, but for all of the 30 years I was in the classroom, a Bible, a dictionary, and various other books were on each teacher's desk. In fact, there were a few times when we actually used the Bible. In shorthand, for example, there was a story which included the word "manna." Many students were not aware of the story in the Bible about manna, the food miraculously provided to the Israelites in the wilderness.

When my first son arrived, I was given a Storkline chest-of-drawers by the faculty. I still have it. When I retired, the faculty presented me with a plaque and a silver serving tray as was customary. The faculty also gave me the nicest bridal shower when I got married. You can see why I have fond memories of the many teachers I got to know and love through the years.

Jerrene and Lewis Martin, colleagues of mine, were also my friends. Jerrene and I shared many problems common to those who have teenagers. She was a home economics teacher and even today I call her with questions about cooking and sewing. It's really nice to have an expert on whom you feel free to call. The late Lewis Martin was a unique individual and I mean that in a very complimentary way. I recall that when he started building his "mansion" a few miles out from Epps, in the middle of forty acres of very beautiful woods, I remarked, "Lewis, why not build on the vacant lot next to ours and you could walk to school?" His reply was, "I can't stand city lights!" Remember Epps is only a village with one traffic light. Many still miss his solos in church. He had a beautiful voice.

Mr. Leonard Rhymes became the agriculture teacher when my friend "Miller" retired. He was so very helpful to me when the business department was mandated by federal guidelines to fill out the many forms required when receiving vocational money. And I always thought income tax forms were complicated!

When asked how she coped with three boys, a certain lady in our community commented to a teacher friend of mine, "Well, I tell you, Mrs. Holmes, you have to pray a lot, whip a lot, and cry a lot!" I only had two sons, but through the years I found her sage advice to be helpful. At my age now, with grown sons and teenage granddaughters, it seems that some sort of crisis is always brewing.

I've recently discovered that, in addition to prayer, something else is very helpful to me. To paraphrase Scarlett O'Hara, I simply say, "Well, fiddle-dee-dee! I'll think about that tomorrow. After all, tomorrow *is* another day."

I keep in my billfold a grandmother's prayer for all occasions: "Dear Lord, please help me to know exactly how my grandchildren should be brought up--and to keep it to myself."

REFLECTIVE REFLECTIONS

When I reflect upon my life, what I find most remarkable is that God chose me to encourage others. As I have already stated, I did not plan to be a teacher, but I am truly happy that I became one. Probably we have been underpaid, unappreciated, harried and overworked at times, but we gained our pay in secret satisfaction. In my particular field, many of my students have gone on to their careers with the skills they learned in my classes. Many have been motivated to go on to college or trade schools majoring in the business subjects I taught. All of my students have touched my heart. Helen Keller said, "The best and the most beautiful things in life cannot be seen or even touched--they must be felt with the heart."

"Teachers are those who use themselves as bridges over which they invite their students to cross, then having facilitated their crossing, joyfully collapse, encouraging them to create bridges of their own." *Nikos Kazantzokis*

Dan Valentine, a veteran newspaper columnist who wrote a column for the Salt Lake City Tribune, says "A teacher is many things--She's knowledge with a smile on her face--Democracy with a book in her hand--Wisdom with a flick of chalkdust on her left eyelid--She's the future of the nation--Love with a college education. Secretly, she will admit 'I have the greatest job of all...' And she has--Because she holds the history of the world in the palm of her hand--She's a teacher!"

Other thoughts I would like to share include this wisdom on being a *Success*, by Harry Emerson Fosdick: "To laugh often and much; to win the respect of intelligent people and the affection of children; to earn the appreciation of honest critics and endure the betrayal of false friends; to appreciate beauty; to find the best in others; to leave the world a little better place than we found it, whether by a healthy child, a garden patch or a redeemed social condition; to know even one life breathed easier because you lived. This is to have succeeded."

"He has achieved success who has lived well, laughed often and loved much! *Bessie Anderson Stanley*

I like this one on *"The Art of Giving"*:

"Remember to be gentle with yourself and others. We are all children of chance, and none can say why some fields will blossom while others lay brown beneath the August sun. Care for those around you. Look past your differences. Their dreams are no less than yours, their choices in life no more easily made. And give. Give in any way you can, of whatever you possess. To give is to love. To withhold is to wither. Care less for your harvest than for how it is shared, and your life will have meaning and your heart will have peace."

On having *Worth:*

"After a while you learn the subtle difference between holding a hand and chaining a soul.

And you learn that love doesn't mean leaning and company doesn't mean security.

And you begin to learn that kisses aren't contracts and presents aren't promises.

And you begin to accept your defeats with your head up and your eyes open, with the grace of an adult, not the grief of a child.

And you learn to build all your roads on today because tomorrow's ground is too uncertain.

After a while you learn that even sunshine burns if you get too much.

So plant your own garden and decorate your own soul, Instead of waiting for someone to bring you flowers.

And you learn that you really can endure--that you really are strong.

And you really do have worth."

Author Unknown

Mark Twain said, "Life is just one darn thing after another."

Will Rogers said, "--live so that you would not be ashamed to sell the family parrot to the town gossip."

"The Roses of Today: One of the most tragic things I know about human nature is that all of us tend to put off living. We are all dreaming of some magical rose garden over the horizon-- instead of enjoying the roses that are blooming outside our windows today." *Dale Carnegie*

94

And then a very favorite of mine, *The Station*. I think as one gets older this essay means more. Enjoy!

THE STATION

Tucked away in our subconscious minds is an idyllic vision in which we see ourselves on a long journey that spans an entire continent. We're traveling by train and, from the windows, we drink in the passing scenes of cars on nearby highways, of children waving at crossings, of cattle grazing in distant pastures, of smoke pouring from power plants, of row upon row of cotton and corn and wheat, of flatlands and valleys, of city skylines and village halls.

But uppermost in our minds is our final destination--for at a certain hour and on a given day, our train will finally pull into the station with bells ringing, flags waving and bands playing. And once that day comes, so many wonderful dreams will come true. So restlessly, we pace the aisles and count the miles, peering ahead, waiting, waiting, waiting for the station.

"Yes, when we reach the station, that will be it!" we promise ourselves. When we're 18--win that promotion--put the last kid through college--buy that 450SL Mercedes Benz--pay off the mortgage--have a nest egg for retirement.

From that day on we will live happily ever after.

Sooner or later, however, we must realize there is no station in this life, no one earthly place to arrive at once and for all. The journey is the joy. The station is an illusion--it constantly outdistances us. Yesterday's a memory, tomorrow's a dream. Yesterday belongs to history, tomorrow belongs to God. Yesterday's a fading sunset, tomorrow's a faint sunrise. Only today is there light enough to love and live.

So, gently close the door on yesterday and throw the key away. It isn't the burdens of today that drive men mad, but rather the regret over yesterday and the fear of tomorrow.

"Relish the moment" is a good motto, especially when coupled with Psalm 118:24, "This is the day which the Lord hath made; we will rejoice and be glad in it"

So stop pacing the aisles and counting the miles. Instead,

swim more rivers, climb more mountains, kiss more babies, count more stars. Laugh more and cry less. Go barefoot oftener. Eat more ice cream. Ride more merry-go-rounds. Watch more sunsets. Life must be lived as we go along. The station will come soon enough.

Robert J. Hastings

Here are a few more of my favorite reflections. I love this next little essay because it drives home the point, in a forceful manner, that each of us is an important part of a bigger picture. Keep this handy and reread it when you get to feeling insignificant. You *do* count. And if you doubt it, read this a second time.

AM I REALLY NEEDED?

Xvxn though my typxwritxr is an old modxl, it works wxll xxcxpt for onx of thx kxys. I'vx wishxd many timxs that it workxd pxrfxctly. Trux, thxrx arx 42 kxys that function, but onx kxy not working makxs thx diffxrxncx. Somxtimxs, it sxxms to mx that our organization is somxwhat likx my typxwritxr--not all thx pxoplx arx working propxrly. You might say, "Wxll, I'm only one pxrson. It won't makx much diffxrxncx." But you sxx, an organization, to bx xfficixnt, nxxds the activx participation of xvxry pxrson. The nxxt time you think your xfforts arxn't nxxdxd, rxmxmbxr my typxwritxr, and say to yoursxlf, "I am a kxy pxrson and thxy nxxd mx vxry much."

It's Spring Today for Teachers, Too!

"Teachers must be dedicated," they say.
Most times I agree, but it's spring today.
Right now, I don't care what great teachers did;
I would rather hop a jet to Madrid,
But here, I'm closed in with wall to wall kids.
     Good grief!
With weeks to go before I get any relief.
The boys grumble and wiggle.

96

The girls mumble and giggle.
Parts of speech, they don't care about.
Spring has arrived and they want out!
How do you think I can teach them proper speech
When spring is here and their interest's beyond
    My reach?
Many facts they do not keep clear,
'Cause their minds are simply not here.
With their friends they are playing somewhere
And about learning they do not care.
They think I am an *"old crow"*
And their feelings don't know,
But how very wrong they are!
I would like to drive my car
Far, far from levels, lessons, and every rule.
It's spring outside and I, too, want out of school!
Mary Pyle Knighten

Educated

IF and AND

If you can hear
The melody of music
In the song
Of a lark at dawn;
And can see the gold
Of a sunset
In the heart
Of a rose,
And if you can see
The destiny
Of a nation
In a group
Of children at play,
And if you
Can feel the throb
Of the heart

Of the world
In the breast
Of a bird,
And if you can
See a tiny star
That swings through space
And gives a bond
For its return,
And in this bond
You recognize
The omnipotent hand
Of Eternal God,
You are educated.

W. P. King

A Teacher's Prayer

Dear Father, hear me as I pray
That every child I teach today
That each small face may be to me
A cherished photograph of Thee--

With patient sweetness let me guide
Each precious soul with love and pride
That when I make their record sheet
No space may be left incomplete--

Then grant me grace, each mind to give
A clear-marked rule by which to live
And then, Dear Father, I beseech
That I may keep the rule I teach!

Author Unknown

"All friendly feelings toward others come from the friendly feelings a person has for himself."

Aristotle

Worthwhile is the saying that a man is a fool who

can't be angry, but a man is wise who *won't* be angry.

Author Unknown

"If the other fellow can make you angry, you have already lost."

Author Unknown

I would like to include a few Classic Teacher Jokes that are favorites of mine.

Before modern day birth control methods, a Cajun couple named their latest offspring "Dammit." A supervisor visiting a teacher one day, heard the teacher say on several occasions. "Dammit," you sit down and be quiet.

Quit raising your hand, you heard me, "Dammit," be quiet. The supervisor stood it as long as he could, then jumped up and said, "Hell, teacher, give him a chance!"

There was a house of ill repute with no elevator.

First Floor: Telephone Operators
Second Floor: Nurses
Third Floor: Teachers

Could not understand why they would climb the stairs to get to the third floor until they heard this conversation:

First Floor: "Number, please."
Second Floor: "Out to lunch. Be back shortly!"
Third Floor: "We're going to get this right if it takes all day!"

A young married man was asked to explain married life. "Well," he drawled, "it's kinda like having money in the bank. You--" (Well, I can't finish this joke as I expect my granddaughters to read this book.) I've always thought a little intrigue makes things more interesting. (Sorry!)

A teacher asked students to go to the board, draw an object and let the class guess what it was:

1st student: Box

2nd student: Blinds on window

3rd student: Flower in pot

4th student: Light bulb

5th student: Woman putting on a girdle

Teachers have class!

Teachers never grow old--they just lose their class!

A hundred years from now--it will not matter what my bank account was, the sort of house I lived in, or the kind of car I drove--but the world may be different because I was important in the life of a child.

Author Unknown.

School is a building that has four walls--with tomorrow inside.

Lou Walters

Good teaching causes scholars to think, to do, to be!

Author Unknown

What we hold in memory is ours forever.

Author Unknown

If I Had My Life To Live Over:

Someone asked me the other day, if I had my life to live over, would I change anything?

"No," I answered, but then I began to think--

If I had my life to live over, I would have talked less and listened more. I would have invited friends over to dinner even if the carpet was stained and the sofa faded.

I would have eaten popcorn in the "good" living room and worried much less about the dirt when someone wanted to light a fire in the fireplace. I would have taken the time to listen to my grandfather ramble about his youth.

I would have never insisted the car windows be rolled up on a summer day because my hair had been teased and sprayed.

I would have burned the pink candle sculptured like a rose before it melted in storage.

I would have sat on the lawn with my children and not worried about grass stains.

I would have cried and laughed less while watching television--and more while watching life.

I would have shared more of the responsibility carried by my husband.

I would have gone to bed when I was sick instead of pretending the earth would go into a holding pattern if I weren't there for the day.

I would never have bought anything just because it was practical, wouldn't show soil or was guaranteed to last a lifetime.

Instead of wishing away my nine months of pregnancy, I'd have cherished every moment and realized that the wonder growing inside me was my only chance in life to assist God in a miracle.

When my child kissed me impetuously, I would never have said, "Later--now go get washed up for dinner."

There would have been more "I love you"--more "I'm sorry"--but mostly, given another shot at life, I would seize every minute--look at it and really see it--live it--and never give it back.

Author Unknown

About Our Attitude:

The longer I live, the more I realize the impact of attitude on life. Attitude, to me, is more important than facts. It is more important than the past, than education, than money, than circumstances, than failures, than successes, than what other people think or say or do. It is more important than appearance, giftedness or skill. It will make or break a company--a church--a home.

The remarkable thing is we have a choice every day regarding the attitude we will embrace for that day. We cannot change the past. We cannot change the fact that people will act in a certain way. We cannot change the inevitable. The only thing we can do is play on the one string we have, and that is our attitude.

I am convinced that life is 10% what happens to me and 90% how I react to it. And so it is with you--we are in charge of our attitude.

None of us can control other people in our lives. Nor can we control the outcomes of situations or events. But we can control our attitude.

Interestingly enough, a supportive, upbeat attitude can be more powerful than a secretly harbored expectation. Such an attitude helps build a positive self image, and seems to guide people toward better and greater achievements.

Author Unknown

Children Learn

If a child lives with criticism,
He learns to condemn.
If a child lives with hostility,
He learns to fight.
If a child lives with ridicule,
He learns to be shy.
If a child lives with shame,
He learns to feel guilty.
If a child lives with tolerance,
He learns to be patient.
If a child lives with encouragement,
He learns confidence.
If a child lives with praise,
He learns to appreciate.
If a child lives with fairness,
He learns justice.
If a child lives with security,
He learns to have faith.
If a child lives with approval,
He learns to like himself.
If a child lives with acceptance and friendship,
He learns to find love in the world.

Dorothy Law Nolte

One of my daughters-in-law calls me a packrat, but I much prefer to be called a collector. I really feel for my sons when it becomes their lot in life to get rid of all of Mom's things. I do collect elephants. It all started when we were first married and my mother-in-law gave me the coffee table and end tables that Bo had brought from Africa on one of his excursions. They are hand-carved solid mahogany and are really a conversation piece.

Since then, I've added a few elephants to my small collection. Some are pieces of jewelry and many have been gifts. Bo's grandmother gave me the pair of ebony bookends he brought back from Africa. I also honestly could open an art gallery of pictures of my grandchildren.

I've traveled to some extent, twice on overseas trips. We took our sons on several trips, including an extended six-week trip one summer. For the last several years, I've really enjoyed the many reunions of Bo's army unit. They are held all over the United States. I've made some really good friends.

Actually, I've really not done anything spectacular! I just hope my life has counted for something in my small corner of the world.

And, I've written this book!

It's a woman's prerogative to change her mind and I did just that about the title of this book. It took several months to come to that conclusion. After considering several other titles, I went back to my original thought *Telling Tales Out of School*. This way it is different from the Reader's Digest's "Tales Out of School" article which they have used for the last four years.

After telling a favorite cousin, Mable, that I had considered the title *Class, May I have Your Attention, Please!*, she remarked, "But I thought you teachers always said *sit down and shut up!*" This reminds me of a teacher I had who always started class by saying, "Sit down, shut up and spit out your gum!" Each and every day this was our greeting.

COLLABORATIVE CHALLENGE

I challenge all my former students to drop me a note. This includes my extended summer classes, my night classes, and also those who audited my classes. I would truly like to know what each of you are doing, what your career choices were, who you married, how many children and grandchildren you may have, and what they are doing. I'm sure it would boggle my mind to know of the many outstanding successes most of you have achieved.

Surprise me and do that! Reading all your notes would add many pleasurable hours to my life. I could even write or compile a sequel to this book and call it *Dear Teacher*. Not only I, but many of your classmates would enjoy this information. I'm getting such good feedback on this thought! Students, simply say what you wish, with confessions (good or bad) and your maiden name signatures. I promise I will compile it as you write it--no edits and no more "nameless students" for intrigue.

We'll simply tell it like it was! I wonder if I should have said that? I hope to hear from all of you!

THOUGHTS ON TEACHING

As I reflect on my teaching career, I think I have gleaned a few valuable thoughts on teaching. I've learned that teaching others teaches the teacher. Also, one needs to possess the patience of Job. Just learn to keep a little patience in your pocket.

If I was successful, I believe it was because I observed these rules or conditions:

- ♦ Learn to ignore some remarks and incidents and they tend to go away. Quite often the student is really seeking attention and when you ignore the situation, the battle is won.

- ♦ Treat all students the same. Human nature dictates that you naturally will like some more than others--but never show any partiality.

- ♦ Always grade fairly. If you feel led to give some student an extra point, explain to the class and give all an extra point.

- ♦ My grade book was always open to my students and they

could average their grades at any given time. This only backfired once.

♦ I believed tests were to be a learning experience and I always returned the tests and we went over them in class. There have been times when a question could be interpreted in a way I was not thinking and out of fairness I would give the student credit for the answer. Quite often, I had students return the tests. Years later, I used the same test again. And, yes, the tests were graded in a timely manner! There are good tests and there are bad tests, and the teacher should learn to ask only what she has thoroughly covered in class. I used a few standardized tests, printed by the company, but they did not carry as much weight as my own tests. I'm a wee bit leery of teachers who always use workbook tests.

♦ There are times when you need to have a private conversation with a student who needs an attitude adjustment. It always worked for me! In fact, one time I challenged a certain boy to make the honor roll for me. He did, and his mother told me later that she felt that he passed because of me. (Now, he did not make the honor roll each time, but he could have.) The point is, he quit misbehaving in my class.

♦ Be friendly, smile (even when you don't feel like it), joke a little, and then get down to business.

♦ There have been times when not only I, but my colleagues as well, would come to school taking antibiotics for a cold, etc., rather than miss a day of school. I always seemed to get so far behind when I did have to miss.

♦ I believe that we as a group were more dedicated to our students' learning than some teachers seem to be today. Notice, I'm not calling any names, just some observations of mine. A few former (good) students came back to teach with us with a complete "attitude" change. I don't know who is to blame, whether it is college or society as a whole, but I saw it happen-- certainly not to all, but to some.

♦ Back in the '50s, '60s and '70s, I believe discipline was maintained partly by the way the teachers dressed. No, we did not look like we stepped off Fifth Avenue, but you could walk down the halls and tell the teachers from the students.

♦ I had a coach tell me one time that when he took his boys out of town to a ball game or tournament, he had them wear ties with their ball jackets. He said they were on better behavior when dressed in this manner. (Proves my point, doesn't it?)

♦ I believed in encouraging students rather than criticizing them. Actually, I seemed to get more work out of them by using this method. If you try hard, you can find at least one thing that deserves a compliment. "If you want to gather honey, don't kick over the beehive."

♦ You need a great love or compassion for your students. Most of my teaching career was in schools where I had small classes and got to know not only the students well, but their parents also. In many cases, the student had problems at home or no encouragement was offered. I learned we can't *think* ourselves into a new way of acting, but we can *act* ourselves into a new way of thinking. When we act lovingly toward others, we ultimately will begin to love them. The hardest ones to love are the "unlovely."

♦ One should know one's subject matter. When you are in your chosen field, in my opinion you are more productive and happy. I had a few "off" courses as I

107

called them (out of my field). Even the age group you work with is different. Once I had an 8th grade English class, followed by a senior class of bookkeeping students. I found that I became "Dr. Jekyll and Mr. Hyde." My heart truly goes out to those teachers who, for various reasons, are not put into their chosen fields.

♦ Do attend the extracurricular activities and become involved with the students you teach on a different level. They notice when you attend their ball games, plays, banquets, etc., and I think they work harder to please you in the classroom.

♦ I think students respond better to consistency. Do not punish one day for something you allow on another day. You are sending mixed signals and, in my experience, that doesn't work.

♦ Let the students know from the beginning what the rules are. Do not keep adding on or omitting as time goes by. Again, you are only sending mixed signals.

♦ Never pretend to know something you really do not know. It will only get you in trouble. Help them look up the question in mind and they will respect you for it. Teachers can be wrong too.

♦ I always wore earrings and still love them today. On very rare occasions, when I really was not feeling well and would not have any earrings on, I was told later that they knew not to cross me on those days. (Never underestimate your students. They know exactly when *not* to push your buttons and also when they can.) Never issue an ultimatum that you do not enforce. This backfired one time in Epps.

♦ In my opinion, another rather controversial thought I have on teaching is simply stated: too much too soon!

No, I do not believe one can learn too much and I know that learning or education is an on-going process. I believe it should be. As Ann Landers' famous quote says, "Use it or lose it." I believe it applies equally to our physical bodies and to our intellectual and spiritual selves. But when a kindergarten student comes home with so much homework there's no time for play, to me that's too much! I have a friend, Junita Rhymes, who taught my granddaughters, and I asked her, "When are they supposed to build a sand castle or climb a tree?" She commented, "We just have to cover so much material."

♦ No, I'm not blaming our teachers. It has been mandated from the parish or state level. I have a good friend, Lou Miller, who for many years taught second grade and taught both my sons. She had taught her own son in a previous year. She told me she threw five times more subject matter at my two sons than she covered when she taught her own son ten years earlier.

♦ Through the years in dealing with teenagers, I learned to listen, not to preach! Give advice only when asked. Of course, for those of us who *know everything*, that is sometimes hard to do. I recently read that teenagers do not come to you to be "preached at" for they can buy a newspaper and read Ann Landers and Billy Graham for that. They simply need you to listen.

♦ I was flattered recently when a young man from our community, whom I had met through my sons, came to me in a state of deep despair. He said he really needed someone older to talk with and he knew me through my sons and felt that I would not mind. Actually, I could not give him much advice, but he talked and I listened calmly and loaned him a book to read. He returned to chat with me several times. I take no credit, but he has really turned his life around and seems to be a very happy young man now. This emphasizes my advice that as teachers, sometimes the best admonition is to simply listen.

♦ In my opinion, a good teacher never assumes anything. Quite often, a student does not comprehend because we teachers just assume that a fact or principle that is so very clear to us is also clear to the student. When we explain thoroughly, our reward quite often is to hear someone say, "Oh, I *see* that now" or "*Now* it makes sense to me."

♦ I still believe in the American Dream. I think we teachers should instill in our students the fact that if they work hard, they will be rewarded when they grow up.

♦ Do you know who is watching you? Someone is always watching how you do your job, how you speak to others and how you control your emotions. Of course, for a teacher, that someone is a student. Will they see a good example to imitate? It's up to you! It's quite a challenge.

♦ A teacher should be a "people person." Be approachable, courteous, respectful of your students' feelings, fair (never showing partiality), stern but not overly strict, and you'll be glad you chose teaching. It is fulfilling and I loved it.

♦ As they progressed to junior high, I told my sons and students that if they could get through eight to ten subjects a day (with most teachers requiring homework), high school would be a breeze.

♦ As I mentioned earlier, I believe too much too soon gives the students early burnout. That's why I found it harder and harder to motivate my high school students. Of course, let's face it, TV is much more entertaining than school (though some television, of course, is very educational). Somewhere along the line, a lot of students needed to be entertained, because not too many were really interested in learning. I hope that now that computers and TV are in common use in the classroom, maybe this burnout phase has improved. For the students' sake and for our future, I sincerely hope so.

♦ I have an opinion on homework, but I've probably said enough already!

♦ Teaching encompassed many phases and facets in my life. I like to think of them as my seasons of teaching:
Spring was when I was young, inexperienced and new at the job. I found it to be a vibrant, though stormy season, when nature was bursting with life.
Summer brought a warmth to my experience. I became more confident in my ability.
Autumn was the time for harvest and it was encouraging to see the fruits of my labor.
Winter must not be forgotten! Yes, the darkness of winter surfaced when I felt "snowed in" by all the demands.

♦ I'm not sure I've covered all the bases upon which I could comment, but I do have one more important piece of advice and that is to have a sense of humor, have a sense of humor, have a sense of humor, have a sense of humor, have a sense of humor!

♦ Yes, teaching is many splendored things!

MEMORABLE MEMENTOS

Of the innumerable things that may evoke memories of our school days (classes, teachers, tests, friends, laughter, books, field trips, banquets, parties, ballgames, carnivals, plays, working on the school paper and annual yearbooks), there is

111

nothing so thoroughly, so absorbingly evocative as a picture.

> "How cruelly sweet are the echoes that pictures start
> When memory plays an old tune on the heart_"
>
> *Author Unknown*

The few snapshots and mementos in my book are intended to do just that, for among so many happy school days, there are sure to be some that hold thoughts rich in memories for each of you.

I still have some copies of the *Panther Tales*, a collection of pictures and a few movies, but plan to use only the comments from the backs of pictures. (I simply could not use all of them.)

And from my unique collection of mementos, I've selected a few of the choice pieces to include in my patchwork quilt of memory. I hope you will enjoy them.

AUTOGRAPHS (RHS, JMD, EHS)

RHS (1947-1948)

Only one yearbook, *The Palmetto*, was published. A few autographs from this book are included on the next four pages.

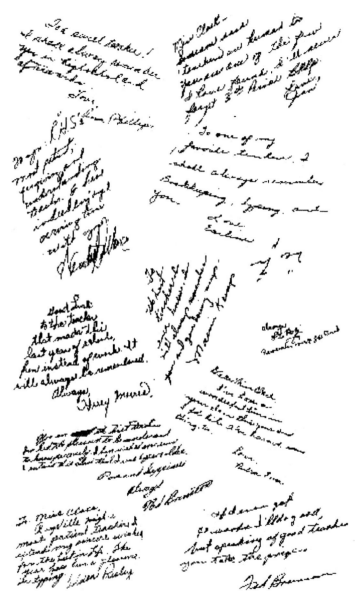

RAYVILLE HIGH SCHOOL

113

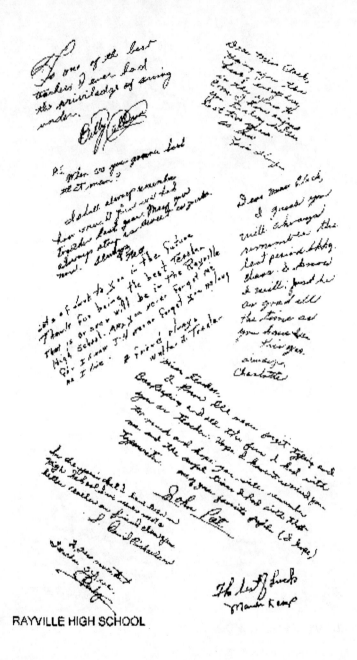

RAYVILLE HIGH SCHOOL

114

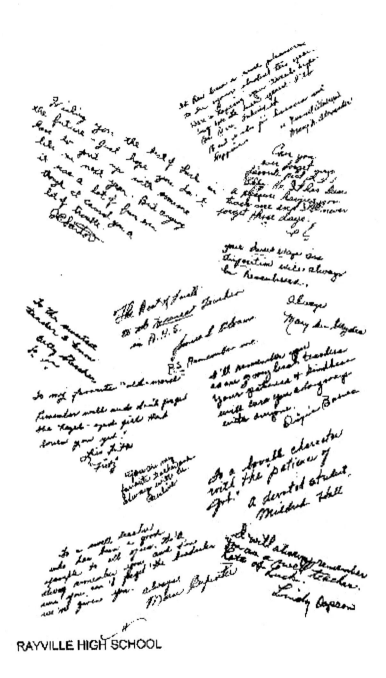

RAYVILLE HIGH SCHOOL

115

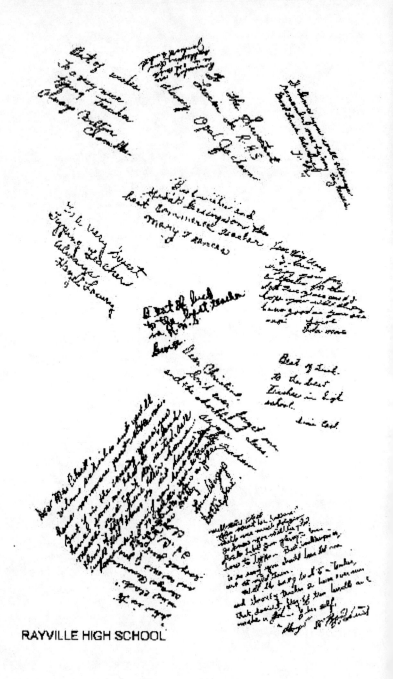

RAYVILLE HIGH SCHOOL

116

JMD (1949)

We had no yearbook and I did not intend to include any pictures, just autographs from the back. Due to the fact that years ago I pasted these few pictures in a scrapbook and then removed them, all autographs were destroyed. I also apologize for parts of the pictures that were ruined. I wanted to include you students in my book so you will be the only school to have your pictures included (see next page).

Joseph Moore Davidson Class of 1949

118

There was no way I could include 27 years worth of pictures. I'm sure many have been lost or misplaced, but I do want to acknowledge those with autographs.

I have a box full of pictures, but had to draw the line somewhere. I simply could not include all of them. So, I decided to include only the autographs from the pictures that had them (see next four pages).

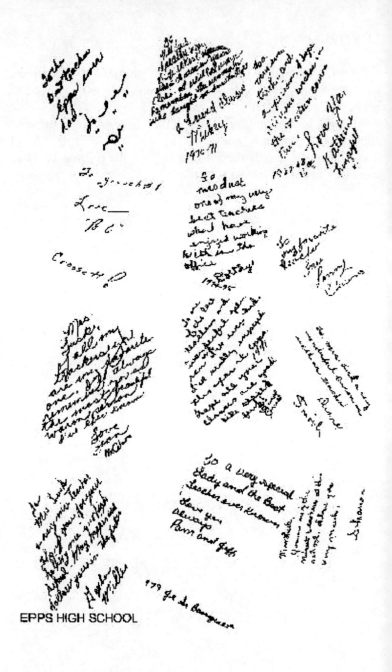

EPPS HIGH SCHOOL

120

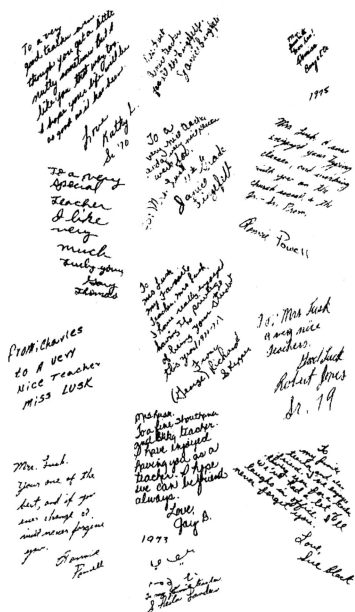

EPPS HIGH SCHOOL

EPPS HIGH SCHOOL

122

EPPS HIGH SCHOOL

123

BANQUETS

In retrospect, I suppose it would be safe to say that the banquets my junior classes and I gave were really "my cup of tea." I got to know and work with the students on a different level outside the classroom setting, and I truly had fun.

They allowed me to choose the Master or Mistress of Ceremonies and I was never disappointed in a single one. I also divided each class into four categories: Program, Invitation, Food and Decoration. Each group worked independently of each other, yet the entire class was involved in the overall job. For instance, the decoration committee planned the decorations and ordered the items we could afford, but the entire class helped to decorate the school cafeteria where the banquet was usually held.

So after lunch on the day of the banquet, the fun and work would begin! Sometimes we just barely had time to rush home, dress and return to become host and hostess to the seniors, teachers and other invited guests. I truly have one big regret. The cafeteria ladies quite often did most or all of the cooking and it never dawned on me or my class to invite them or the janitorial staff who were also very helpful. I use this means to apologize for this oversight.

The day after the banquet, we cleaned up the cafeteria, returned all tables and left it in "tip-top condition." I have many pictures of this clean-up task. Can you imagine Doug Fairchild and Walter Sidney Hillman mopping the floor?

I have many pictures and a few movies of the actual banquets. Some of them, in fact most of them, were so pretty! We always carried out a theme in our decorations and programs and through the years had many nice compliments. We always had an entertaining program, including the traditional Junior Prophecy and the Senior Class Will. Some of these were really clever! My program committee gave this prophecy top priority and kept it a secret even from the rest of the juniors. That way it was always more of a success and interesting to all. We really "fixed" some students with this prophecy, but it was all in fun. I never knew of anyone getting offended. Actually, through the years and quite by accident, a prophecy or two came true.

Traditionally, sophomores served for us and would agree to dress appropriately for the theme and put on a skit. They must have enjoyed it because we would have a waiting list of volunteers each year.

On the old "town books" was a law forbidding dancing within the town limits. I know that was true for I've been told that years ago my own mother-in-law was turned out of the Baptist church for dancing. One year, without asking the mayor for permission, our principal told us we could try, so the prom was added. Behavior was good and we got to have several without being reprimanded. In fact (and my students know this), many of the teachers would intentionally go home early, even including the principal. I must thank Coach Mac (Henry W. McPherson) for staying longer several times. The students would be having such a good time they would beg me to stay a little longer. My husband Bo helped me to chaperone many times until midnight. In fact, my students thought as much of Bo as I hope they did of me.

I shall never forget one party we chaperoned when the limbo was popular. Bo won the contest, beating high school boys much younger.

The banquet became the social highlight of the school year. It was so nice to see the students all dressed up in grand attire. They didn't have to wear long dresses, it could be short Sunday frocks, but it finally became formal with long gowns and rented tuxedos. For a "one-redlight town," this was really an event. Sometimes we could afford musicians, but mostly a record player was used.

In keeping with the theme of the year, we always obtained background music which related. If the desired record could not be obtained locally, I discovered we could order from Randy's Record Shop in Gallatin, Tennessee, to get the exact song we wanted.

You can tell from reading the above that it was truly an enjoyable job for me, but also a time-consuming one. I would get behind on paper grading and also on the two sets of books I kept for the office.

There have been a few times when I would go to Mr.

Gilmore after the banquet and say, "I need a rest; let someone else do this next year." He had a way of convincing me that truly no one else could do such a good job and I would leave his office conned once more into another banquet for another year. This was to happen 15 times in my 27 years of teaching there.

In the years from 1950 to 1956, we were given $50 with which to put on the banquet. We made our own programs and all the decorations and costumes. It is truly amazing to me what one can do with crepe paper, corrugated paper, and a few innovative minds. The school always picked up the tab for the food, which was usually cooked by the cafeteria ladies.

Believe it or not, I actually have a list of these banquets with their themes and, in many cases, their exact cost. Also listed are my very capable MCs. I have included a few of the actual comments that I had written on the yellowed sheet of paper I found. May you reminisce and enjoy!

1950--Hawaiian; MC Fred Wilson

1951--Colonial Plantation; MC William "Bill" Crow

1952--Moonlight and Roses; MC P.M. Alexander

1953--Dew Drop Inn; MC Millard Thornton

1954--The Last Round-up; MC Johnny Guice (held in the gym)

1955--Starlight; MC Larry Shows

1956--Over The Rainbow; MC Ruth Thornton (The banquets listed above cost $50 each)

1957--Tropicana; MC Bill Smith (If I recall correctly, it rained, thundered and the wind blew, giving us a lot of atmosphere). Cost: $72.14

1958--Fairyland; MC Ben Rider (had party at Murphy's Lodge). Cost: $68.33

1959--Paradise of the Deep; MC Kenny Thrower. (I was on maternity leave. Miss Martha Till, who took my place, sponsored the banquet).

1960--Oriental Gardens; MC Homer Plunkett (held at Frontier Village in Delhi; knife incident).

1961--With A Song In My Heart (I was on another maternity leave. Miss Joy Holly, who took my place, sponsored the banquet).

1962--Wonderland by Night (banquet and prom); MC Paul Mercer. (The very best banquet so far.) Cost $170

1963--Magic Moments (banquet and prom); MC Gary Miller. (Good also.)

1964--Red Sails In The Sunset (banquet and prom); MC Allen Hendrix. Cost $141.76

1965--Rendezvous in Spain (banquet and prom, sponsored by Erline Jones); MC Max Reeves. Held at Country Club in Delhi.

1966--In The Misty Moonlight (banquet and prom); MC David Jones. (the prettiest ever.) Approximate cost $300, cost of band $75.

1967--Paris By Night (prom only). Sponsored by Jessie Lee Hillman.

1968--A Night In Las Vegas (banquet and prom); MCs Donna Ratliff and Mike Sewell.

After this year, Carolyn Kirkpatrick was *honored* with the job of sponsor. It was truly nice to attend as a spectator only.

At one banquet when the "Twist" was in its prime, all were having a really good time. You did not really need a partner, so the dance floor was crowded. One girl who had a heart problem was one of the many who were dancing. A student, Mary Margaret Davis, came to tell me that Mary Lee Hines was out of breath. I went to talk to her about resting for a while. She never stopped "doing the twist" as she said to me, "Mrs. Lusk, I don't care if I fall out--I'm having so much fun, I'm going to dance till the music stops." She danced all night with no ill effects.

I can't be certain, but I have a suspicious feeling that one bowl of punch was spiked at my last banquet, "A Night In Las Vegas." I'm not accusing anyone, simply making a statement. No doubt I'll be told if this was true or not. Through the years, many confessions have been made after the fact--when it was too late to do anything about them!

The Pearl-Handled Peril. In 1960, our banquet theme was

Oriental Gardens, and to do something different, we held it at the Frontier Village in Delhi, a neighboring town. The owner had to use a set of his personal steak knives, which held great sentimental value to him. On Monday morning, he called the school about missing knives. What was I to do? Three were missing. Not knowing who took them or who might know anything about them, I pondered the situation. I'm happy to say my method worked. I called a meeting of the juniors and seniors who were in attendance and the sophomores who were the servers. I did not fuss or accuse. "Don't we all know of people who take souvenirs from hotels?" I commented. I told them I did not approve, but that I felt that the knives may have been taken as souvenirs. I explained how much they meant to the owner and gave this request: "In the morning, I hope to see all three knives on my desk. I don't even want to know who took them, but I believe they will be on my desk in the morning." Guess what, they were! To this day, I don't know who took them.

I was always given a very beautiful corsage by the junior class.

The invitation committee had fun with the place cards. Usually, the teachers sat together and the junior and senior students were mixed. This was kept a secret until the night of the banquet. Actually, we take credit for seating two together who then started dating and later married. They were Bill Collins and Sarah Tatum. Couples were always paired and the committee made up some couples. I seem to think we started another romance by seating two together. I can't put a name to the couple unless it was Paul Mercer and Sherry Neal.

I received a nickname one year and it stuck for the entire year. Allen Hendrix told the class one day at a class meeting to be quiet as "Mademoiselle" wanted to speak. It was later shortened to "Madam." I told them that one connotation of Madam was not necessarily a complimentary one. It seems we were contemplating a banquet theme around a Paris theme, and although Red Sails In the Sunset won out, Madam stuck. Even now, some of these students call me Madam. I'm sure I was called names much worse. I wish I knew!

One year, in order to create the atmosphere we wanted, we turned off most of the lights and used candles. Another year, we taped the wall switches in the off position. Both years, Mr. Gilmore would have someone go and turn on all the lights. So the next year, we unscrewed the bulbs and got the atmosphere we wanted. Mr. Gilmore never mentioned it to me, but I'm willing to bet that he knew what we had done.

I recall the banquet that Annie Ruth Gwin, Jackie Tharpe and many others were involved in. They actually voted to work on the banquet after class so as not to miss any of my classes. Hard to believe, isn't it? I'm sure it took some of my family time, but even I did not get behind in my work at school.

We had speakers at several banquets, but not at all. Those I remember were Lucy Williamson, a retired schoolteacher, Fern Barden from Oak Grove and Dean Bill Smith from Louisiana Tech University in Ruston. They all gave nice motivational speeches. I recall one speaker, who shall remain nameless, who went on and on and on. We learned to put a time limit very quickly. The one all enjoyed the most was a local humorist, author and businessman from Monroe, Harry Addison. He actually kept us in stitches!

Truly, to see my students in dressy outfits made it hard for me to believe that they were the same ones in my classes day after day. And in my opinion, when they were all dressed up, somehow they were on their best behavior. Another regret I have is that parents did not get to see their sons or daughters perform, whether in a skit, song, reading the prophecy or will, or just simply being gracious hosts and hostesses. I tried to instill in them the proper etiquette for an event of this kind. Needless to say, they all made me *very proud!*

BULLETIN BOARDS

When my department in the new building was under construction, I requested and got an extra large bulletin board.

Sometimes students were in charge of a display, but usually I kept it updated with posters on special projects we were studying. I liked to use jokes or funny cartoons to stress projects in which we were involved or to get across important concepts.

One use of the bulletin board was to have my typing classes compete against each other on speed tests. A little friendly competition always improved their speed--somehow, they tried harder.

Maybe you will remember our trip to Key West by typing speed in the cold winter months (To Florida or Bust) or Have Speed, Will Travel (patterned after the then current TV show "Have Gun, Will Travel"). I also remember when Russia launched Sputnik. If they could, we could too, so we "Shot For The Moon." The students were strictly on their honor as they progressed to the final destination. For the most part, they were honest. The losers had to buy cokes for the winning class and I furnished the cookies. The bulletin board display did not have any bearing on their grade, other than that it boosted their speed quite a bit.

CARNIVALS

Who can forget the instrumental rendition of *Fascination* used for the Beauty Pageants? During the many years that Erline Jones and I were in charge of the Carnival, we used this music as the King escorted his Queen and Maid down a ramp extending into the gym.

I have only a partial list of these winners. I found the following list in my grade books. Possibly these eight winners represent the years I was involved with the Carnival.

    1954   King--"Red" Cawthon
            Queen--Maxine Traxler
            Maid--Vivian Corley

    1955   King--James McGuffee
            Queen--Ruby Farrar
            Maid--Doris Roberson

    1956   King--Kenneth Blackwell
            Queen--Patricia Butts

Maid--Linda Hale

1962   King--Mike Newton
          Queen--Jeanette Weatherly
          Maid-- Ruby Kitchens

1963   King--Mitchell Hillman
          Queen--Jami Jones
          Maid--Kathaleen Walters

1964   King--Wayne Tanner
          Queen--Jeanette Hale
          Maid--Nina Powell

1965   Royalty--no Carnival
          King--Jerry Forbes
          Queen--Sue Shows
          Maid--Lindia Smith

          Grammar School
          King--Jimmy Owens
          Queen--Julie Jones
          Maid--Denise Boyette

1969   Royalty--no Carnival
          King--Mike Sewell
          Queen--Judy Oldham
          Maid--Mary Ruth Henderson

If I recall correctly, the Kings, Queens and Maids were selected from each class by popular vote. The winner was the one who could garner the most votes based on monetary contributions. Sometimes these contests became very competitive, especially when relatives wanted their queen to win. But after all, the object was to make money for operating expenses for the school.

These Kings and Queens were found in my collection of yearbooks. I have 13 yearbooks that were published in my 27

131

years at Epps. I also seem to recall that a Carnival was not held every year.

1951   Grammar School
Halloween King--Kenneth Morris
Halloween Queen--Cherry Hawkins

High School
Halloween King--Douglas Fairchild
Halloween Queen--Juanita Ball

1952   Grammar School
Halloween King--E. V. Roberts
Halloween Queen--Annie Ruth Gwin

High School
Halloween King--J. L. Smith
Halloween Queen--Betty Jo Raley

1953   Grammar School
Halloween King--Louie Cleveland
Halloween Queen--Jo Henson

High School
Halloween King--Harlan Tanner
Halloween Queen--Wanda Rose Prine

1959   Grammar School
Halloween King--Mike Jones
Halloween Queen--Mary Margaret Davis
Halloween Maid--Carolyn Weatherly

High School
Halloween King--Larry Hale
Halloween Queen--Ann Williams
Halloween Maid--Glenda Stroud

1961   Grammar School

Halloween King--Mike Brister
Halloween Queen--Candy Jones

High School
Halloween King--Ken Newton
Halloween Queen--Vera Hale Newton
Halloween Maid--Gerrie Simms

JUNIOR CLASS OFFICERS
(a very incomplete list)

1950   President: Fred Wilson
        Vice-President: Morris Ray Plunkett
        Secretary: Maureen Young
        Treasurer: Dorothy Adams
        Reporter: Colie Powell

1951   President: Betty Jo Raley
        Vice-President: Sam Crawford
        Secretary-Treasurer: Yvonne Coats
        Reporter: Bonnie Simms

1954   President: Sara Jo Calhoun
        Vice-President: Johnny Guice
        Secretary: Maxine Traxler
        Reporter: Mary Ford

1955   President: Deek Johnston
        Vice-President: Jimmy Holmes
        Secretary-Treasurer: Toni Newton
        Reporter: Peggy Trim
        Parliamentarian: Nelda Leach

1956   President: John Mercer
        Vice-President: Ruth Thornton
        Secretary-Treasurer: Jean Sealy
        Reporter: Ruby Farrar

1957　President: Patricia Butts
　　　　Vice-President: Glenda Thrower
　　　　Secretary-Treasurer: Linda Hale
　　　　Reporter: Voncille Ezell
　　　　Historian: Bonnie Farrar

1958　President: Mildred Hendrix
　　　　Vice-President: Margaret Reeves
　　　　Secretary-Treasurer: Patsy Collins and Glenda
　　　　　　Richmond
　　　　Reporter: June Coody
　　　　Parliamentarian: Ben Rider

1960　President: Ken Newton
　　　　Vice-President: Brian Weatherly
　　　　Secretary-Treasurer: Gerrie Simms
　　　　Reporter: Louise Black and Douglas Rider
　　　　Parliamentarian: Sherman McMillan

1962　President: Paul Mercer
　　　　Vice-President: Mike Newton
　　　　Secretary-Treasurer: Ruth Kitchens
　　　　Reporter: Judy Simms

1963　President: Jimmy Coleman
　　　　Vice-President: Timothy Miller
　　　　Secretary: Maxine Charleace Hinton
　　　　Treasurer: Benny Tannehill
　　　　Parliamentarian: Charlie Smith

1964　President: Joe Gilmore
　　　　Vice-President: Jo Ann Simms
　　　　Secretary: Carolyn Simms
　　　　Treasurer: Wayne Tanner
　　　　Reporter: Linda Kay Coody

1969　SENIORS (I sponsored the senior class this year.
　　　　Why? I don't recall):

134

President: Connie Carter
Vice-President: Ronald McDermitt
Secretary-Treasurer: Mary Ruth Henderson
Reporter: Judy Oldham

CLUBS

Youth For Christ
Gladys Holmes, Sponsor

Beta Club
Erline Jones, Sponsor

Future Homemakers of America (FHA)
and Future Farmers of America (FFA)
Sponsored by the Home Economics and Agriculture
Departments
Lela Jones and Jerrene Martin
C. L. Miller and Leonard R. Rhymes

Future Business Leaders of America (FBLA)
Chris Lusk, Sponsor

Civic Club
Sponsored by current teacher at the time.

English Club
In several of my English classes, we had individual clubs.
We usually joined a Pen Pal Club. Seventh and eighth graders
enjoyed this activity and many kept their pen pals for years. I
just wonder if any still are in contact with one another. It would
be interesting to know.

English Classes of Chris Lusk.

Student Council
This organization existed for a few years.

Chorus
Mrs. Doris Buckley, music teacher

FUTURE BUSINESS LEADERS OF AMERICA

I tried to organize this club many times previously, but we were actually chartered the school year of 1977-78. As I retired in 1979, I did not get the club involved in activities on a district level. We did participate in the parish "Anything Goes Olympics" and brought home a second-place trophy on our first try. We later won a first-place trophy. It was a lot of fun for everyone, both participants and spectators as well.

This club kept a scrapbook. I was totally surprised when the scrapbook was dedicated to me and a plaque was given to me with a beautiful corsage of red roses. I am so proud of the plaque. I have it displayed over my desk and have pressed the corsage to keep as a souvenir.

FBLA Officers
President: Connie Gwin
Vice-President: Pam Lingefelt
Secretary: Lisa Simms
Treasurer: Cecil Ratliff
Historian: Anis Martin
Reporter: Lisa Scriber
Parliamentarian: Larry Lusk

Committees
Program: Diane Hale and Denese McCalmon
Projects: Anis Martin and Vickie Mobley
Ways and Means: Julie Nielsen and Robin Fryer

GRADUATION

Hold On To The Moment
Single file and yet together,
we've shared our greatest days.

And we carry common memory
In different ways.
Though we don't know where we're going,
We will cherish where we've been.
I want to cry. I want to shout--
Want to let this feeling out.
Hold on to the moment. Let the feelings show.
Hold on to the moment. Never let go.
I can picture us together with my arms around my friends.
Just let me hold on to this moment, before it ends.
There was laughter. There were tears,
through the dozen golden years.

Author Unknown

Graduation is so many things, it's laughter, smiles and
    cheers.
It's speeches, songs and warm applause.
It's fond farewells and tears. It's handshakes, hugs and
Compliments from family and faculty.
It's lingering memories of the past and plans for days to be.
Graduation is so many things all wrapped up into one.
A dream fulfilled, a milestone crossed,
A bright new life begun.

Author Unknown.

Believe it or not, as a teacher I usually find graduations sad.
I'm proud and sad at the same time. You see, we teachers can
become attached to some of you students as much as your
friends can. Experience teaches us that many years may pass
before our paths cross again and sometimes they never do.

"I have always liked teenagers, the fresh way they look at
life and their free and easy style. I like their confidence, their
courage, their optimism. I like the way they walk--limber and
free and friendly. Young people--with tomorrow in their eyes. I
like teenagers.

"This statement always startles my senior citizen friends.
Anyone past 65 is not supposed to like teenagers. Tolerate them,
yes. Love them, of course. But like them, never!

"But I like teenagers! Their very youth makes teenagers pioneers. They think over mountains. They are the future of the world with young hope in their hearts. Bright faces, eager smiles--alert eyes--energy in motion." (Paraphrased from *I Like Teenagers* by Dan Valentine.)

Through the years of working with teenagers, they have kept me young-at-heart. And with the different ages of my granddaughters, Taffy (17), Brent (13), Elizabeth (9), Emily (7), and Mary (2), I plan on their influence on my life keeping me young-at-heart for many years. I'm thankful for my teenagers and those who will become teenagers. I'm looking forward to being young-at-heart. Never an old fogey, not I! Morally speaking, I suppose I will always be an old fogey. My heart and mind cannot accept the moral standards so prevalent today.

MISCELLANEOUS

I was able to retrieve the desk that I used in my office at school for approximately 22 years before it was trashed. Prior to my using it, Mr. Gilmore used this same desk in the upstairs office of the old two-story high school building for approximately 25 years. It was there when he first became principal in 1931-32. So it is at least 75 years old and my husband and I both have fond memories of it. He remembers when he had to lean over the desk and have the "rubber tube" applied to his posterior. It occupies a place of prominence in my den and I use it almost every day.

I also retrieved an old wooden chalk box that has quite a bit of history attached to it. A letter I received from the Dixon Ticonderoga Company in 1997 had this to say: "The American Crayon Company was the largest manufacturer of wooden boxes in the world during the first half of the 1900s. When corrugated fiber board (cardboard) boxes became available, the cost associated with wooden boxes became prohibitive. Wooden boxes were manufactured by the American Crayon Company through the forties. After W. W. II, production was stopped." I also have a pair of the metal bookends that were used in schools for years.

My office helpers and I cleaned out and re-organized the book room. Mr. Segars said I could have anything I wanted that we no longer used. I regret not getting the old, old Underwood typewriter that I first used in the office. It was so old that the entire carriage came up when you shifted for capitals. Talk about needing strong fingers! There was also a wooden framed wall clock that was no longer being used that I now wish I had retrieved.

I donated to the library all of the English newspapers pertaining to the coronation of Queen Elizabeth of England. They were sent to my husband by the English lady in whose home he stayed just before his unit embarked for the beaches of France. I wonder if those papers still exist.

A scholarship fund was set up by former students and was given in honor of the following teachers: C. L. Miller in 1996, C. W. Gilmore in 1997. I think this gesture was quite an honor!

Teachers' aides I remember with fondness were Mable Jackson, Nanita Weatherly and Geraldine Coleman.

Pelican Girls State was awarded each year by the Ladies Auxiliary of the American Legion. The girls' names I found were: Margaret Reeves, June Coody, Nina Powell, and Jo Ann Simms. I know there were many more, I just could not find any information on them.

We entered the Ruston Rally, which gave us regional competition for a couple of years. Mary Margaret Davis and Gary Miller placed first in Typing I and Judy Simms placed in shorthand.

Quite often, at the end of the school year, I awarded pins to the three best typists. Later on, a "Golden E Certificate" was awarded at graduation to the outstanding Business Education student. Sorry, but I do not have a complete list of all who received them.

A very incomplete list of the highest speeds obtained for the years shown:

1955	Patricia Ezell	66
	Toni Newton	65
	Geraldine McPherson	57
1956	Ruth Thornton	71
	Sammie Lane Dickens	70
	Robin Newton	69
1957	Glenda Thrower	67 2/5
	Bill Smith	67 1/5
	Pat Tanner	56
1958	Margaret Ann Reeves	58
	Mildred Hendrix	54
	Wayne Holley	53
1967	Phil Jackson	72
	Gary Crouch	70
	Terry McKnight	63
1968	Connie Carter	74
	Rusty Prine	74
	Vickie Prine	73
	Rusty Kitchens	65

> These speed averages were based on 3 and 5 minute test scores. Much higher speeds were attained on 1 minute "sprints for speed" and also on the repetition of the famous sentence "Now is the time…"

Speed Demons

Herman Bell	56
Lisa Cawthon	62
Cindy Corley	65
Donna Gwin	62
Fay Hall	54
Kay Hall	52
Terri Hillman	61
Julie Jones	69
Kim Kitchens	59
Daryl Lusk	51
Annette Runions	69
Dawn Waller	65
Brenda Brock	60
Erma Brown	55
Brenda Day	52
Connie Gwin	60
Alvin Johnson	53

George Lewis	61
Anis Martin	50
Julie Nielsen	60
Bobby Runions	63
Ronnie Corley	84
David Hogan	61
Mike Sewell	64
Alan Simms	60
Clifton Wingfield	71
Karlene Cook	65
Bruce Franklin	60
Paul Gowan	70
Joycelyn McDermitt	75
James D. McPherson	84
Max Reeves	63
Craig Hale	58
Richard Brock	60
Ronnie Jackson	65
Rhonda Chelette	61
David Jones	63
Ronald Lingefelt	75
Brenda McCalmon	59
Pam Oliphant	77
Janice Owens	73
Glenda Prine	66
George Rider	71
Sue Black	65
Cheryl Brister	55
Diane Collins	55
Mary R. Henderson	50
Allen Latch	56
Karen Prine	52
Brenda Sue Hale	71
Bonnie Holly	81
Raymond Lingefelt	78
Linda Matthews	69
Randy Miller	70
Johnny Simms	66

| Janie Carter | 65 |
| Sandra Gowan | 59 |

Other Speed Demons

I know there were quite a few others whose speed would qualify them to be called "speed demons," but after our guidelines changed, speed did not count as half of their grade. Production counted and speed was not emphasized as much as accuracy.

Sorry, I do not have the highest speed recorded. Possibly it was posted to a separate sheet of paper and not placed in my grade book.

Other Business Awards

Sorry, once again I do not have a complete list.

1964: Monroe Office Equipment of Monroe named Mary Margaret Davis "The Best Typist of the Year."

1965: Certificate of Business Education Award to Mary Margaret Davis and Jeanette Hale.
Certificate to Wayne Tanner who learned touch on ten-key adding machine. He was my only student to ever receive this award.

1978: "Golden E" Award to the following:
BOOKKEEPING
Janet White
Donna Roberson
CLERICAL PRACTICE
Darrye Clark
Loretta May
Erma Brown
SHORTHAND
Erma Brown

1979 CLERICAL PRACTICE
Richard Hillman
Leonard Rhymes
BOOKEEPING
Leonard Rhymes

TYPING I
Laney Rhymes
Marsha Harris
Sonja Fox ↙
Mary Martin
Mary Beth Beard
Debra Collier
SENIOR AWARDS (Golden E)
BOOKKEEPING
Julie Nielsen (all A's)
Jimmy Jones
Cheryl McPherson
Robert Jones
CLERICAL PRACTICE
Anis Martin (all A's)

FBLA State Spelling Contest (500 words)

Charleace Hinton won a certificate for spelling 500 words correctly! Girls missing only one word on state spelling contest were: Jackie Tharpe, Annie Ruth Gwin, Robin Newton and Alice Sherman.

Accuracy Awards Given by Facit Corporation

In the annual Facit Accuracy Contest in typing, Gary Miller and Jami Jones won medals. These awards were given to students who completed a perfect copy of a pre-arranged pamphlet distributed by the Facit Typewriter Corporation. I received three of these awards; other winners were June Fryer and Eileen Butler.

PALS (just a few I remember)

Glenda Thrower and Patsy Tanner
Dot Adams, Helen Guice and Marcie Kitchens
Juanita Ball and Peggy Felker
Annie Ruth Gwin and Jackie Tharpe
Toni Newton and Sue Sealy
Donna Roberson and Janet White
Rose Jones and Wanda Smith

Avie Nell Kennedy, Mary Ford and Lillie Lou Hall
Erma Brown, Darrye Clark and Loretta May
Louise Black and Lula McCandlish
Lisa Hale and Connie Plunkett
Sarah Segars and Kathy Lingefelt
Fran Tharpe and Yvonne Hale
Joe Gilmore and Allen Hendrix
Butch Thrower and Jarvis Thomas
Laney Rhymes and Bruce Johnson
Paul Mercer and Don Raley
Mary Margaret Davis and Sue Shows
Jimmy Copes and Joe Gilmore
Ray Hemphill, Sam Crawford and Fred Wilson
Sybil Polk, Maurice Nelson and Wanda Rose Prine
Loretta Brock and Billie Ruth Crnkovic
Gay Whitaker and Bobbie Jean Brock
Byron Boykin and Gary Neal Crouch
Claudine Hemphill and Wilma McCurley
Craig Hale and Malcolm Butler
Ruby Kitchens, Edyth Hale and Karlene Cook
Barry Cook, David Hogan and David Weatherly
John Mercer and Larry Ball
Maxine Traxler and Syble Young
Evelyn Beasley and Lois Hale
Gwen Miller and Janie Tannehill
Robin Black and Annette Runions
Daryl Lusk, Andy Johnston and Gerald Talley
Larry Lusk, Curt Ryals, Cecil Ratliff, Rusty Maples and Phillip Parker
Craig Yates and Larry Lusk
Lewis Martin and Daryl Lusk

Those who said "I Do" before graduation
Penny Prine Chowns
Vicki Jones Yates (Clyde)
Lula Hendrix Russell
Gladys Marie Derrick Bunyard
Leathie Crawley White (Burlen)

144

Dana Simms Gwin (Carl)
Bertha Simms Powell (Tommy)
Linda Matthews Hale (Craig)
Rhonda Brock Prine (Rusty)
Gayla Hale Miller (Randy)
Rise Miller Fallin
Sherry Butler Hillman (Stevie)
Vera Hale Newton (Ken)
Bonnie Weatherly Hawsey (Kenneth)
Peggy A. Felker Dunn
Ann Skipper Boykin
Paula Jackson Hough
Brenda Hall Brown
Yvonne Coates Hale
Brenda Sue Hale Herrington
Becky White Plunkett (Dobbin)
Alice Varner Neal
Geraldine McPherson Fox (Sonny)
Ann Hickman Hillman (Mitchell)
Brenda Sue Hedricks Young

Does it get any wilder than this?

"Simply tie yourself onto a one-ton, big-horned, thrashing slab of slobbering, muscle-bound beef, then tell the guy next to you to open the gate 'cause you want to see if you can ride this thing around the arena for eight seconds or so." I've always thought that anyone who wants to ride one-and-a-half to two tons of bull has an elevator that doesn't go to the top floor.

Bull riding isn't for everyone! But for several years, my husband did just that. It was before I knew him, thank goodness. I'll have to say that I've attended more than my share of rodeos with him.

That's why one class at a recent reunion had me riding a bull in their graphics. I looked for someone seated at a typewriter, but they did it their way. The joke was on me, but I enjoyed it.
I did, however, pull a terrible prank on Doug Fairchild. He was responsible for the bull-riding teacher, so one Christmas I gave him a free certificate for one visit to Dr. Kevorkian. I thought if

anyone could take the joke, he could. Well, weeks went by and no comment from him. I was beginning to think that I had hurt his feelings. Then, after letting me *sweat* for about three weeks, he thanked me for the gift and said, "I went to see him, but he turned me down because I was so good-looking and so many Epps women depend on my weekly hugs." I lost again!

Gifts received

When I got married, the faculty gave me a very nice bridal shower. When my first son arrived, the faculty gave me a Storkline Chest to match my baby bed. I still use the chest and all of my granddaughters and some nieces and nephews have also used the baby bed. Lou Miller's grandson Sean also used it when he visited in his grandparents' home.

When I retired, the faculty and staff presented me with a plaque for 30 years of teaching service and a beautiful silver tray.

Timeline of my life at school

In researching and compiling all of this information, it was a staggering realization to me to find out how many students I have been associated with during my 30 years of teaching. I can only give a rough estimate, but it exceeds 2000 individuals. This includes my regular classes and the four years that I taught an extended class. In the '50s, I held night classes for Ouachita Valley Vocational School of Monroe. The classes were held here at Epps, but I have no idea how many years or how many students were involved. I've called their personnel department and they do not have it in their computers, hence I can only give an estimate.

I kept a register for 26 of my 27 years at EHS. For 26 of the years, I sponsored the junior class as well as 15 banquets.

During the years of 1974, 1975, 1978 and 1979, I taught extended classes in the month of June. Of course I was paid extra for these added months, as I was for my night classes.

1947:   Taught at Rayville High School in Rayville, Lousiana. I was 19 years old. I kept my first study hall. My aversion to study halls began.

1948: Rayville for another year, still on a T-certificate.

1949: Joseph Moore Davidson High School in St. Joseph, Louisiana. A truly *fun* year.

1950: Epps High School in Epps, Louisiana. Had my first register, sponsored my first junior class, and gave a banquet. Also had my first PE class.

1951: Sponsored the first school paper. My one and only junior play.

1952: Another study hall. Miss Clack became Mrs. Lusk!

1953: Another PE class.

1954: Moved into my new department in the new high school building. Worked in the office two periods a day. Was given my own office and desk.

1958: Mr. Segars became principal. I had three office periods.

1959: Maternity leave.

1961: Maternity leave.

1965: Sponsored my first yearbook.

1969: Sponsored the senior class for the first time.

1970: Integrated grades 9-12.

1971: Integrated grades 1-8. Received vocational money for first time. Would receive for two more years.

1972: Mr. Don Gwin became principal. I had four office periods. Mable Jackson became an aide and helped in the office. I taught only bookkeeping and shorthand. I might need to add that I was never paid any extra money; the office periods were simply counted as one or more of the six hours of classes we had per day.

1974: Volunteers and I put out a yearbook in honor of the first graduating class of Epps in 1925. Celebrated the 50th Anniversary of EHS.

1975: Taught journalism and sponsored both a yearbook and school paper.

1976: Taught journalism again. Sponsored yearbook and paper.

1977: Took a sabbatical. Mable Jackson was hired as school secretary. New grammar school building (grades 1-7).

1978: No office work.

1979: No office work. I had six classes, but no extracurricular activities other than my FBLA Club. No register for the first time at Epps. This was my *countdown* to retirement. I retired in 1979 at age 52 with 30 years of teaching experience. I thoroughly enjoyed my last year of teaching!

During the years that are not listed, I sponsored the junior class, we put out editions of the school paper *Panther Tales,* we gave a junior-senior banquet, I kept a register, and I also worked in the office for at least two periods. Just wanted you to know that I didn't "goof-off" during those years.

Night classes

All vocational schools in Louisiana are now called Louisiana Technical Colleges, and the one in West Monroe is called Delta Ouachita Campus (formerly Ouachita Valley Vocational School). Back in the '50s, I taught night classes for a number of years, and of course I didn't keep a list of the years or the names of those I taught. Many adults from surrounding areas attended, as did a few high school students (even though they did not receive credit for the course taught). To the best of my knowledge, this was done in the '50s in The Barn, and I also remember holding classes in the present high school building which was first occupied in 1954.

Shorthand, bookkeeping and typing were taught. For some it was a review, for others completely new material. It was a challenge and a lot of work to have students on various levels, but when an adult gives up six hours of family life at night, it just naturally inspires the teacher. And, I might add, I was paid for my work.

Extended classes

I taught an extended summer program, a vocational business program, at Epps High School in the month of June in 1974, 1975, 1978 and 1979. Persons eligible were adults and those not presently enrolled in high school. I was shocked when I discovered that I had taught Erline Jones. She and I became good friends when I first married into the family and remain so today. We've had many good times together.

From a teacher's standpoint, it was a real challenge to teach those who displayed such an interest. These summer programs were good for my ego. I discovered I really could teach when I had students who wanted to learn and I didn't have to waste time on discipline.

In shorthand class, all the brief forms were introduced. The entire phonetic alphabet, all word beginnings and endings, and techniques of the phrasing principles were covered. Some years, we were able to cover the entire "reading" phase of shorthand and an introduction to writing was begun. Some years, for some individuals, the class afforded a review, and they were able to

149

progress to the level of dictation by records, transcribing into mailable letters.

One summer, Edith Kitchens and Lizzie Lee Crouch covered in a month the two shorthand books that we normally covered in a school year. Now, we didn't do much writing, nor did we take dictation. We just read several lessons a day. It was such fun to have those who really wanted to learn. They were both really good!

The correct key locations and proper posture and stroking techniques were emphasized in typing. The ability to prepare typewritten copy conforming to accepted standards of form and arrangement were learned. We briefly touched on all phases of letter writing, including vertical and horizontal centering. Some time was also devoted to typing forms and tabulation, and manuscript typing was introduced. We certainly did not have time to stress speed. Again, it was a real challenge to have students at all levels. Some summers, I had to introduce the keyboard.

We were able to cover the bookkeeping cycle twice in its simplest form and a somewhat thorough business vocabulary was learned. Touch control of ten-key adding and calculating machines was introduced. Proper check writing hints were introduced and students were taught how to reconcile a bank statement. Some members of this class were interested in setting up a simple system of records for their husbands' businesses. Using this as a teaching tool benefited many as they actually saw how a system of record keeping is begun by using step-by-step procedures. This project also provided a balance to bookkeeping theory, served as a drill on principles, and made use of application problems.

Some summers, I invited former students now involved in a business job to briefly speak to the class. I also had demonstrations of current office machines and equipment and displays of supplies from local office equipment firms. Many students were thoroughly interested, even to the extent of asking for homework. They remained in class from 7 am until 1 pm and never seemed to tire. They wanted to cover as much material as possible and we truly "traveled double time."

I had some old bookkeeping texts I could give them, and I got permission to give them the two Practice Sets that accompanied the textbook. I also invited them to call me at my home if they needed any help. Yes, it was a lot of work, but as a teacher, it was so rewarding. I thoroughly enjoyed working with and getting to know many of the adults from our community who attended these classes.

During my extended classes, I got to know and work with many adults of the community, both black and white. One of my favorite black students was Sally Mae Kelly. She took typing and bookkeeping from me and I helped her with a set of books she was keeping for some organization in the parish. She said to me, "Miss Chris, I remember Mr. Bo when he was in diapers. We go back a long way!"

Nice notes

On the following two pages, I've included a few of my favorite notes that mean so much to me. I've misplaced some and I'm truly sorry as I would love to have included them.

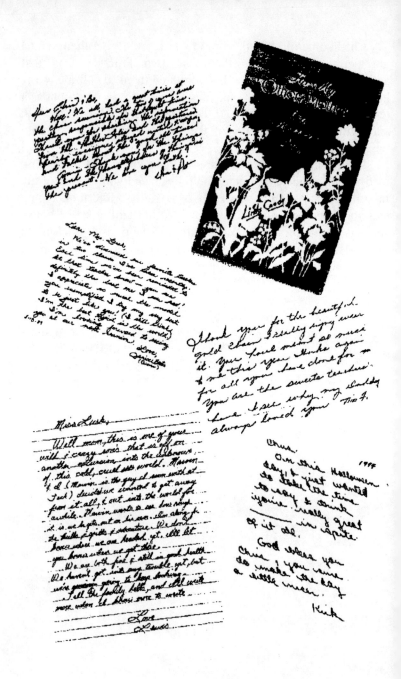

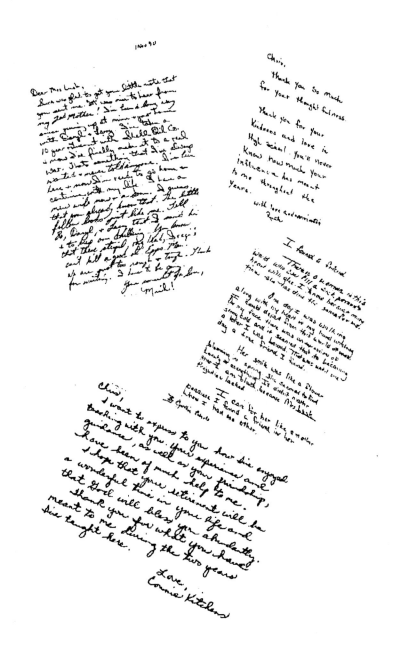

PANTHER TALES

The 1951 seniors were my very first class to publish a school paper. I seem to recall that it was called *Panther Prowl* then and later renamed *Panther Tales.*

Editor	Marcelain Kitchens
Assistant Editor	Sibyl Ann Gilmore
Gossip Editor	Maurine Young
Art Editors	Billy Leach and Ruthie McPherson
Feature Editor	Helen Guice
Sports Editor	Fred Wilson
Poetry Editor	Ray Hemphill
Organizational Editor	Dorothy Adams
Faculty Advisor	Miss Clack
Reporters	John Plunkett
	Elda Glynn Lewis
	Minnie Lou McPherson
	Bertie Jean Hale
	Morris Ray Plunkett
	Bill Collins
	Buddy Calcote
	Charles Dickens

Others editors in later years were as follows:
   Toni Newton (most innovative)
   Maxine Traxler (paper renamed when she was editor)
   Mary Margaret Davis
   Jeff Fox (Journalism Class)
   Lynn Fryer (Journalism Class)
   Joycelyn McDermitt and Max Reeves (co-editors)
   Wayne Holly
   Gary Miller
   Raymond Lingefelt
   Donna Hogan
   Glenda Thrower
   Dennis Trim
   Ruth Thornton

I'm sure that I do not have all copies of the *Panther Tales* that we published. Occasionally, the paper staff would be omitted from an issue. Some years a paper was published every six weeks. So this list is as accurate as possible. I remember the days on which the paper was issued (usually costing five cents). Hall duty was a breeze! The students were either sitting on the floor or leaning on their lockers, all reading the paper. To some the gossip section was the best.

In 1975 and 1976, I taught journalism. One of our projects was to have a paper staff and put out issues of the *Panther Tales*. I expected more and better work for these editions, as they had class time to do the job and were actually graded on the issues. In previous years, it was just worked into a regular typing class or the students used a free period to work on the paper. I was pleased with all my editors, but Toni Newton gets special mention. She was innovative in giving the paper a three-column layout, which actually resembled a real newspaper. This certainly gave much practice on the correct division of words. To my dismay, several errors slipped by. Remember, though, these years represented extracurricular activities on the students' part. They also had to keep up with their assigned work in typing.

Journalism Class paper staffs

1975	Editor	Lynn Fryer
	Assistant Editor	Janice Prine
	Organizational Editor	Charles Johnston
	Assistant Organizational Editor	Julie Jones
	News Editors	Kathy Ratliff
		Becky Swett
	Copy Editors	Stephanie Walker
		Sharron Carter
	Business Managers	Debbie Monroe
		Dorothy Collins
	Special Editors	Lovely Bams
		Ora Adams

155

Reporters	Kathy Nielsen
	Sarah Henderson
Artists	Melverta Brown
	Brenda Barnes

1976	Editor	Jeff Fox
	Organizational Editor	Sue Ratliff
	Reporters	Denise Boyette
		Debra Barnes
		Billie Ruth Day
	Typists	Becky Swett
		Kathy Neilsen
		Sarah Henderson

Categories I had to omit

In several issues of the *Panther Tales*, I found popularity contests. Realizing it would not be feasible to publish all of them, I simply wish to comment on the one that most impressed me. Of the 16 categories to be voted on, Henry Newton won eight and Pat Butts won five. Jean Sealy captured two. All other winners won in only one category. This included grades 9-12 and the individuals were voted on by their peers. Quite an honor, don't you think? Also, several times a popularity contest was held to pick the "Ideal Girl" and "Ideal Boy" of EHS. Again, it simply was not feasible to put all of them and I didn't want to pick out only one.

My granddaughter saw this one particular popularity contest and commented, "Nanny, you are included in the categories, so I want you to include this one." You will learn, if you haven't already, that a grandchild is the boss! For her sake, as well as because I am proud to be listed, I will include only this one list:

Campus Sweethearts: Pat Butts and Henry Newton
Cutest: Mildred Williams and T. J. Williams
Mr. and Miss EHS: Henry Newton and Bonnie Farrar
Best All Around: Pat Butts and Henry Newton
Most Likely to Succeed: Jean Sealy and Henry Newton
Most Popular: Pat Butts and Henry Newton

Best Athlete: Marianne Kitchens and Larry Ball
Most Intelligent: Jean Sealy and Bill Smith
Best Dressed: Glenda Thrower and Wayne Pickett/Henry
    Newton
Wittiest: Marianne Kitchens and John Mercer
Quietest: Mary Leach and James Tarver
Loudest: Margaret Reeves and Sheldon Ezell
Flirtiest: Mavis Edwards and Edward Holley
Ideal Girl and Boy Friend: Pat Butts and Henry Newton
Best Sport: Pat Butts and Henry Newton
Cutest Smile: Robin Newton and E. V. Roberts
Best-Liked Teacher: Christine Lusk and B. R. Davis

Songs of the Month or Song Dedications were sometimes a feature of different issues of the paper. Several were very clever.

Sports! I've heard it said that if all the basketballs deflated, we would have to dismiss school! Yes, sports were an integral part of our school system. I believe our sports program kept many youngsters in school and involved in their classes. Later on, baseball was to become very important, and much later track was added.

Our teams won many games and tournaments, both on the local and district level. A few teams made it to the state level. At times, my paper staff had clever headings for this column. For example, "Sports and Facts with Bud and Jack."

Someone should compile and publish the records set by our athletic teams through the years.

Gossip! Yes, it was included in each issue of the paper. I tried to edit the entire paper and especially this part to keep from offending anyone, but I was never too successful. For example: "What were ET, MAB and CR doing the other night? How about this, BC?" Or "What is the reason LKE and JEM broke up? Could it have been BO?" or "JC, WK and LS know it all, don't they, girls? Ask BT or BM!" They knew, but I certainly did not! Oh well, no one was actually *shot* over the gossip columns. A few names I recall for this column were "Snarls by Kathy and Charles," "In the Know with Joe Ann and Joe,"

"Gossip Scoop by Ruth the Snoop" and "Coke Break with Red and Snake."

And who can forget our assembly line when stapling the paper together?

Each year, as I have already mentioned, we had the traditional Junior-Senior Banquet. Always included were the Junior Prophecy and Senior Will. I always thought the students did a superb job on these. I could not print all and simply could not pick out only one.

After the banquet, the gossip section really had lots to tell about the banquet highlights. I've really enjoyed reading these. Many took me back in time several years and I chuckled quite often.

In some issues of the Panther Tales, they included "Meet the Students" and "Meet the Teachers." These were most interesting. Another feature was "Plans of the Seniors."

Sometimes the paper staff would put out special editions for holidays. One year they began to sell ads to local merchants and always wrote clever jingles pertaining to the participating businesses. This money was used to help defray costs involved in publishing a paper. We always tried to include Grammar School News in each issue of the paper, and club news and current events were usually covered very thoroughly. (This section is continued in Afterthoughts.)

PANTHER TRACKS

In my 27 years at Epps, 13 yearbooks were published. They were not published every year. This was due in large part to the financial condition of the school at the time. The years that yearbooks were published were 1951, 1952, 1953, 1959, 1961, 1965, 1969, 1974, 1975, 1976, 1977, 1978 and 1979.

Why no autographs? The yearbooks never arrived until the beginning of the new school year.

In my two years of teaching Journalism (1975 and 1976), class time was used to work on both the yearbook and the school paper. When Mr. Gwin realized that 1974 would be our fiftieth anniversary, we decided to honor the 1925 graduates and had them seated on the stage graduation night. We also quickly published a yearbook dedicated to them.

1975 yearbook staff:

Editor	Charles Johnston
Business Managers	Kathy Ratliff
	Stephanie Waller
	Sharron Carter
Class Editors	Janice Prine
	Becky Swett
	Sarah Henderson
	Kathy Nielsen
Sports Editor	Lynn Fryer
Activities Editors	Dorothy Collins
	Melverta Brown
	Brenda Barnes
Academic	Lovely Bams
	Ora Adams
Photographers	Julie Jones
	Debbie Monroe

1976 yearbook staff:

Editor	Denise Boyette
Business Manager	Sue Ratliff
Art Editor and Photographer	✓ Jeff Fox
Copy Editor	Debra Barnes
Organizational Editor	Billie Day
Staff	Becky Swett
	Kathy Neilsen
	Sarah Henderson

(This is continued in Afterthoughts.)

PLAYS

I only sponsored one play, "The Adorable Imp." This was a junior play and was probably in 1951. I thought the class did really well, because I certainly did not know what I was doing. Later after I was married, my husband Bo always attended plays with me. My students told me that they knew they were talking loudly enough or "getting the point across" when they could hear him laughing.

Sorry, I could not find a list of the play characters. I remember a few, but to be fair I won't list any of them.

RETIREMENT

This is a copy of the speech I was finally coerced into giving on graduation night in May 1979. I also handed out awards that night, the same night my second son graduated.

"In reflecting on my years of teaching as my retirement draws near, I have so many people to thank for making this phase of my life the richest and most satisfying--actually the best years of my life!

"First, I would like to thank my mother. She is here tonight. I am grateful to my mother and dad for guiding me and insisting that "their girls" get a college education. That is why I am a teacher and here tonight.

"Also, thanks go to my husband and sons. Without their cooperation and understanding, I simply would not have made it--as any working mother can vouch.

"Thanks to Mr. W. L. Gwin for establishing a business department here and to all the principals, colleagues, faculty and staff with whom I worked, for the friendship and comradeship we have. There is an affection between us that only people who work together can understand.

"Thanks also to the parents and the people of this Epps community who have through the years cooperated with me, encouraged me, and allowed me to become their friend. I feel that I have made a few friends who love me even though they know all my faults.

"Now last but by no means least, I want to say thanks to the many students or kids (wonderful "kids") that I have taught! Wonder fills me at all the young people I have come to *know* and *love* through teaching them. They have added something priceless to my life.

"Whenever I would despair of this generation, I have only had to look about me to have my faith restored. I say Thank You, Lord, that there are still so many of our "kids" who are reading, studying, working, practicing and getting an education. Kids who do not abuse their bodies and who are making the most of their minds. Kids who know pretty much who they are and where they plan to go.

"They are made of tougher stuff than we were (they have to be to survive). They know more, care more and are going to achieve more for mankind. They are our *wonderful kids!*

"To paraphrase the beloved American humorist Will Rogers who said 'I never met a man I didn't like'--well, I never met a student I didn't like!"

"Thank you!"

Retirement Speech May 1979

WHO SAYS JOHNNY CAN'T READ?

Newspaper clippings in my files show that nice things were said about our schools. A sampling of headlines from these articles is shown here:

West Carroll No. 1 (March 1, 1979)

Johnny reads better in West Carroll (March 25, 1979)
WC ninth graders are first in state (August 31, 1988)
Three West Carroll Schools receive praise from ACT assessment program (June 17, 1992)
West Carroll students shine (August 12, 1998)

AFTERTHOUGHTS

I failed to mention the nutcracker set that Linda Coody gave me one year. Of course I remember her fondly in the winter months when Bo keeps it filled with nuts--and also scatters the hulls on the hearth and carpet. I also am reminded of her love of my macaroni and cheese dish, which now I cook quite often for one of my granddaughters.

Gaye Whitaker named her daughter Chaylor. I thought that was such a pretty name. I got her permission to call my second child Chaylor; however, my second child was a boy.

I suppose the confession from a former student that boggles my mind the most is the one from Raymond Lingefelt. It was unexpected, flattering and still almost unbelievable to me. It certainly will remain as the one that touched my heart in a very profound way.

Ronnie Corley, the "big flirt," has through the years given me various compliments, as have Don Raley, Buddy Ashley and many, many more.

J. E. Miller recently told Bo and me that he loved me as his favorite teacher very much. He says he never learned to type, but enjoyed my classes anyway! These former students simply amaze me with their compliments.

I recently had to have a series of shots for an allergic reaction to a prescription drug. One day the nurse on duty was Mona Philley. She remarked, "Oh, goody, I get to *shoot my teacher!*"

At the recent 50th reunion of a class I taught in Rayville, I asked Huey Morris if he had received my note. I had previously written him, along with several other people, a thank you note with some other comments included. He told me he still had my note. This was after a span of five years! I found that very flattering and touching. He was always special to me, as was Ned Brunson, a classmate of his.

When a few of my teacher friends and I were talking and reminiscing, we remembered that the thing to do at recess was to get a 5 cent coke, put in a 5 cent bag of salted peanuts and enjoy. Then the game was to see who had a bottle from out-of-state. The winner was the one whose city and state were the farthest away. Sounds like great fun, doesn't it! Remember, life was simpler in the Dark Ages.

I feel I really should not fail to mention Dwain Tharpe in a very special way. We have many shared memories. He was a student of mine, we taught together on the same faculty, and our lives have been somewhat similar in various ways. We still see each other occasionally. He and Bo are friends and I consider his wife to be a good friend.

Jeanette Weatherly told me recently what she remembered most about me. She said, "You really boosted my self-esteem when you suggested to me that I enter our local parish beauty pageant." I was right, too. In my opinion, she is still a very attractive young lady. She said, "I didn't enter, but you surely helped my ego."

Remember that in a way Doug Fairchild was the cause of my considering writing a book. So we continue to give each other gag gifts. The latest I got from him was a plaque which stated *Four things a woman should know: how to look like a girl, how to act like a lady, how to think like a man, and how to work like a dog!* This is my book, so I reserve the right to *not* mention the gag gifts I have given to him. I will say this: I should be ashamed of myself--but I'm not! If you want to know about them, you'll just have to ask him.

Having formerly been a dark brunette, it was a tough decision to let my hair eventually go white. I became so tired of the weekly rinses that I finally gave in to nature. Many like it, but some do not. I know it's a shock to someone who hasn't seen me for a few years.

At a reunion in September of 1998, I received a very nice compliment on my hair. The husband of one of my ex-students said in my presence, "Now see this lady's hair, Earline, that's why I do not want you to put anything on your hair." Buck Baker, you surely boosted my self-esteem and you were probably not even aware of it. Thanks, anyway!

Jean Adams is another student who majored in business education. She taught in the public school system of Ouachita High School in Monroe. She is now retired.

The first yearbook I sponsored was for the school year 1965. We used "Memories" as the theme for the publication.

Co-Editors	Joe Gilmore and Jeanette Hale
Business Managers	Carolyn Simms and Sue Shows
Photographer	Mike Jones
Organizational Managers	Nina Powell and Jo Ann Simms
Sports Editor	Larry Simms
Art Editor	Carolyn Weatherly
Copy Editor	Shirley Duckworth

Once when John Mercer, a former student, was Superintendent of West Carroll Parish Schools, he called me to help him evaluate some curricula and be on a Task Force he was organizing. I considered it an honor to be asked, but I politely refused. I believe one time I was scheduled for surgery and the other time, I was enjoying my granddaughter entirely too much. I should be ashamed for not helping him for he had been one of my favorite "pests." The fact is that when I retired, I truly retired. I never put my name on the substitute list. I truly learned to relax. I thought of myself as "a wet leaf on a log." One cannot get much more relaxed than that!

Margania Hendrix has been working in the business field for approximately 25 years. She is now manager of an insurance company in Monroe. We saw each other recently.

Steve Marshall was in one of my English classes. To me, he was the "Flip Wilson" of EHS. He kept talking one day and finally I said, "Steve, just sit here and look at the pictures in the book and be quiet until the bell rings." On reflection, wouldn't a Rubik's Cube have been handy? That particular day, Bobby Runion said, "Mrs. Lusk, Steve just comes to school to get a free lunch." Instead of causing a "riot," Steve just grinned and said, "That's right, Mrs. Lusk."

We never had an organized PTA at our school, but most parents were concerned and cooperative. I know we had "more privileges" as teachers than did our students. In my opinion, that is the way it should be! I believe this fact helped with discipline in the classroom and on campus. We demanded and received more respect. I also believe that clothes impact the seriousness with which you are taken; different modes of dress command different modes of respect.

I'll always remember the "Hardtack Candy" the Monroe girls gave me at Christmas time. I have the recipe and make it for my granddaughters now. I remember Becky and Debbie fondly when I make this candy.

I'm so proud of Joy Black. She is now attending college with her own daughter.

Some authorities believe that fundamentals of correct usage of grammar apply mostly to formal expression. Now, however, conversational English is in correct usage. For example, it is sometimes correct to use a preposition at the end of a sentence, particularly if it sounds natural depending on the emphasis and effectiveness obtained. Also, if a word or a phrase used parenthetically does not interrupt the thought of the sentence, the commas may be omitted. This usage is more common than in the past. Our English language has now become "The Queen's English." (Information by a recent LSU graduate.) Toni tells me it is no longer called *typing*, but *keyboarding*. Times are changing!

Jo Ann Simms also majored in business, but I do not believe she ever taught in the public school system. I know she taught Vocational Business in a Vo Tech school in Alabama for a few years.

The day I officially retired, I actually entered the hospital for surgery on both feet. Sounds exciting, doesn't it? Yes, I did have those tingling, slow traveling "hot flashes" from time to time. It was very obvious as my face would become flushed. I coped with these by stopping and saying, "Yes, class, I'm having a hot flash. Many of you will understand when you get a little

165

older." After fanning and everyone having a chuckle, it was back to business as usual. No problem!

Glenda Stroud was a delight to have in class. All the boys had a huge crush on her. I recall that at one reunion held in a home, several boys literally threw her into the swimming pool dressed in her casual clothes. Her begging and screaming were to no avail.

I failed to mention a stunt that Mary Margaret Davis pulled on her friends. She gave several of them a piece of what they thought was Hershey candy. They discovered the next day that the carefully wrapped chocolates were really EXLAX!

When I think of Epps High School, I'll always remember this trio: Mr. Henry Johnston, Madeline Johnston and Nellie Waller. They were well-liked, sweet, efficient and friendly to all. I'm proud to have known them.

I wish to mention the many friendly, cooperative and efficient lunchroom ladies that crossed my path while at Epps. They never seemed to mind preparing the food for the banquets and never complained when my students used their kitchen for the clean-up job the next day. They have my sincere gratitude.

Don't all of you agree that Toni did a *superb* job of putting my manuscript into book format for me? Really, you can't conceive or appreciate the vast amount of work that went into this book. The manuscript of mine that she had to rearrange, correct and put into an orderly fashion would not have even rated an "F" if I had graded it. I hope she shreds it!

I had compiled a composite of Panther Tales and we both regret that some items were not suitable for scanning or just came out too bad to use. It covered several issues through the years. I think just the mention of these categories will bring back fond memories for most of you. Some were in each issue of the paper, remember?

I'll try to remember a few of the parts I had chosen:

> First Paper Staff: (Look under Panther Tales)
> Editorial and Comments:
> > Weeds and You (by a reformed smoker)—Allen Hendrix

On Parking?—Freddy Tannehill (No, Freddy did not type it)

The School Patrol—Charles Johnston

School Also Has Fringe Benefits—Raymond Lingefelt

On Tests—Lynn Fryer

Our Great State—Sandra Hale

Evils of Gambling—Don Lockard

A Point to Ponder—Jami Jones

Poems

Yea Seniors—Ray Hemphill

School Days—Jean Adams

Wages of War—Betty Jo Raley

What is a Friend?—Cynthia Roberts

Spring—Wayne Jackson

'Twas But a Dream—Maxine Traxler and staff

Class Room Scene—Ruth Thornton

(some of the above poems were written by these students when they were in grammar school)

Essays

Confessions of a Typewriting Machine

A Boy's Thoughts While Studying Bookkeeping (dedicated to Bubba Kitchens)

Jokes

Several cute jokes (but this one actually happened:)

Mrs. Lela Jones: "When the sauce begins to boil, put in a tablespoon of water."

Ruby Kitchens: "Level or heaping?"

Sports

Of course, basketball and baseball were our main programs and we won our share of trophies. Dobbin Plunkett set an outstanding record in track before we had organized track teams at our school. He won many medals and was invited to New Orleans where he placed second in the state, missing first place by only three feet.

Likes & Dislikes

Several were included, including teachers as well as

students.

Miscellaneous Categories
 What If...?
 Did You Know?
 Try to Imagine
 Seniors Advise
 Happiness Is...
 Excuses, Excuses!
 School Jingles
 Paws & Claws
 Panther Theater
 Coloring Book—Gary Neal Crouch
 Interviews (teachers and new students)—Debbie Monroe
 What's In A Name—Kathy Nielsen and Sarah Henderson
 High School Is—Dorothy Collins

Creative Writing (added the two years I taught Journalism)
 My Grandfather--Brenda Barnes
 Old
 The First Day
 First Time
 (The three listed above were outstanding. I can't recall who wrote them.)

Charter members of the Epps FBLA Club were the following students: Janet White, Terri Hillman, Tina Fairchild, Diane Hale, Donna Robinson, Brenda Brock, Pam Waller, Sarah Mobley, Larry Lusk, Lisa D. Smith, Marsha Harris, Elizabeth Weatherly, Lisa Scriber, Cindy Beard, Cecil Ratliff, Phillip Parker, Leonard Rhymes, Anis Martin, Connie Gwin, Rise Fallin, Robin Fryer, Jody Johnston, Todd Bastion, Richard Hillman, Alvin Johnson, Jimmy Jones and Ivory Lewis. The first year the club and I designated Mr. W. L. Gwin as our first Honorary Member and presented him with a plaque. The year I retired, 1979, I was also made an Honorary Member.

How many of you recall the "yo-yo craze" when the two-story building existed? Several were able to exhibit their skills (by using a very long string) from the second floor to the ground. What a unique sight!

On a rainy day in June, 1999, funeral services were held for Gladys Barr Holmes. In so many ways, however, she will still be with us. She influenced both colleagues and students in a special way as English teacher at Epps High School and we will remember her. One such student is Bill Smith of South Carolina. Apparently someone called him about her untimely death. The next day he called me, obviously upset. (He called Mrs. Holmes quite often and I received calls from him occasionally.) This particular day, he said, "I just wanted to know how you are and how you are feeling. I can't bear to lose both of my favorite teachers. Take care, and I'll call you again in about a month." Now, wasn't that sweet!

I learned why I did not have Kevin in my classes. It was during integration and he said he was assigned to my co-worker. I feel the loss was mine.

After much musing and meditating on this thought, I've decided to include my utmost confession. I'm very fortunate to have been happily married for a long time. After delving back in memory to write this book, however, certain feelings and emotions surfaced. Now that I've received varied compliments and confessions, they have quite often put a twinkle in my eye and a song in my heart. It also put me to thinking that confessions are truly good for the soul.

This is just one bit more of intrigue. I feel I could have become "interested" in one of my students had I been available and had our age difference not been so great. I believe the chemistry would have emerged. I may tell him some day; perhaps I should. My intuition tells me that he will be very surprised. Upon reflection, however, he may recall that he was always very special to me. Now, start guessing!

PAST, PRESENT, FUTURE!

In compiling this information and incidents about individual students, I have diligently tried to include all who should be recognized.

Knowing that I possibly have omitted several, I take this means to apologize for these omissions; they were not intentional. My fervent prayer is that those who read this book will enjoy it and not feel "left out" but instead simply rejoice, as I have, that our paths crossed.

I have instructed my family to ask former students to serve as pallbearers for me when the time comes and *all* are to be named as honorary pallbearers.

A former student, Louie Cleveland, is our music director at church, and recently another former student, James Kitchens, was ordained by our church to preach. I have asked both of them to take part in my "final farewell." May God bestow his richest blessings on each of you.

I sincerely say *"Thanks!"*

ABOUT THE AUTHOR

Christine Clack Lusk grew up on a farm in rural northeast Louisiana near Rayville. In reflecting on her past she recalls that as a little girl playing, she always insisted on being the teacher.

She graduated from Rayville High School in Rayville, Louisiana at the age of 16 with a grade-point average of 3.7, placing second in a class of 73. The scholarship she received allowed her to attend LSU in Baton Rouge, Louisiana. She planned to go into the field of business and work in that capacity, certainly not teach.

During World War II, there was a teacher shortage and her former principal asked her to fill in temporarily for him in the business department. The money was tempting, so after only 3 years of college and at 19 years of age she taught for two years at RHS in Rayville, Louisiana, her alma mater. She found that she truly enjoyed teenagers and usually related well to them. So she became a teacher, really by accident. She states that it was a serendipitous event in more ways than one!

She later married W. A. "Bo" Lusk of Epps, Louisiana, and they have two sons. They have been blessed with 5 granddaughters, who added a whole new dimension to her life. She still lives in the sleepy little village of Epps, Louisiana, where Bogzack creek meanders lazily on the western side.

She states the book TELLING TALES OUT OF SCHOOL, evolved really by accident as the result of a joke. It has been a most pleasant task for her. She dedicates it to all her former students, each of whom have left "footprints on her heart".